basic skills
of oral
communication

Speech Communication Series

basic skills
of oral
communication

Dominick LaRusso
University of Washington

WM. C. BROWN COMPANY PUBLISHERS, Dubuque, Iowa

SPEECH SERIES

Consulting Editor

BAXTER M. GEETING, PH.D.
Sacramento State College
Sacramento, California

Manufactured by
WM. C. BROWN CO. INC., Dubuque, Iowa
Printed in U. S. A.

Dynamic developments of our time, particularly the communication explosion and new revelations concerning human behavior, demand fresh approaches to the teaching of speech. Modern life places an emphasis on speech as an *act of communication*, interdisciplinary in nature, capable of adding new dimensions to man's evolution and progress in all areas of life. The SPEECH COMMUNICATION SERIES, addressed to the introductory student, represents a significant attempt to provide new materials for today's teaching needs.

Basic to all titles in the series is the desire to present the material in the clearest and most lucid style for the purpose of making speech communication a useful, ethical and satisfying experience. While the individual titles are self-contained, collectively they provide the substance for a comprehensive study of those topics fundamental to a basic course in speech communication.

To
YOU
from
me

IMPORTANT TRIFLES

Each year hundreds of young people enter adulthood with little or no ability in the basic patterns of social living. Ironically, more money and effort are spent to repair these abilities than to teach them correctly in the first place. Somehow, within the last seventy-five years especially, the idea of learning to do things "naturally" has dominated education. The thought is that desirable habits of thinking, creating and communicating can be acquired without expending special time, money or effort. Actually, these are among the most unnatural acts of man in that the precise co-ordinations of thought, nervous and muscular reaction are too complex to be acquired by mere growth. Moreover, the demands of modern living require that these habits be refined to the utmost and one who depends upon learning them "naturally" faces serious handicaps. The natural style is as misleading as it is misunderstood.

When athletes speak of a natural style, they do not assume a person who runs, throws, jumps or swims as he did in his childhood. They mean instead, the well co-ordinated and superbly conditioned person who has disciplined his natural strength and rhythm to produce a flowing pattern of movements suited for some particular sport. So, too, when professionals speak of a natural style in communication, they do not mean speech studded with grammatical inconsistencies, conceptual incongruities, contradictions and redundancies. They refer, rather, to speech which is sensitively worded, organized and adapted. Naturalness alone can rarely create such sophisticated patterns of behavior.

But rules alone, likewise, fail to produce masterpieces. While adherence to rules will improve the artistic performance, slavish dedication to them will produce little more than mechanical imitation. Still, a sensitive understanding of successful theory is as important to a potential athlete as it is to a fledgling doctor, engineer or teacher. All sophisticated human activity is best learned through a skillful combination of *theory, model* and *guided practice*. Each is important in its own right, but together they serve to initiate, develop and sustain all the worthwhile activity of civilization.

While all learning of this nature is, at first, ponderous and mechanical, it soon becomes the automatic foundation of future success in all matters from sport to intellect. The miraculous save made by a goal tender in a professional hockey game results from immediate inspiration which releases well-trained habits of the past. The good speaker is one whose spontaneous thoughts, language and delivery result from flexibility inspired by a thorough mastery of rules, directed by good models and insured by guided practice. Truly, success derives from blending nature and art.

This book strives to define the essential ingredients in successful communication. Moreover, it furnishes models and directions for rewarding practice. But the one thing it cannot provide, the one thing that furnishes the key to improvement, is desire. With desire, anyone can improve in anything; without it, all the theory and models available could not produce one iota of change.

CONTENTS

PART III ORAL COMMUNICATION: ACTION AND REACTION

PART I

ORAL COMMUNICATION
Proportion and Detail

*Our Speech reveals the height, depth
and width of our lives.*

Chapter 1

NATURE OF
COMMUNICATION

It should be commonplace that human civilization would not be possible without communication. Since societies are formed by the interaction of individuals, and since this interaction is more symbolic than physical, some system of sharing desires and fears must be part of man's civilized traditions. That system, conceived in faith and nurtured by man's strong need for companionship, is *symbolization*. It remains the single greatest achievement of mankind — atom bomb and guided missiles notwithstanding.[1]

By realizing that he remained alone unless he could translate his experiences to himself and to others, man endeavored to convert his experiences into symbols. As a result of symbolization, man for the first time could get beyond the limits of his physical being and, thereby, leave the animal class. In the beginning, symbols were very closely associated with the thing they represented. In written form, early symbols were actually attempts to represent objects — diagrams of men, animals, the sun and the like. In oral form, most of the symbols were onomatopoeic (they sounded like the thing they sought to represent). Obviously, individual members of such primitive societies were quite limited in their ability to share experiences and desires. When group interaction became more precise and regular, as relationship or value needed representation, symbols increased in number and complexity. With this change, alphabets were constructed and rules regarding their use gradually found their way into the traditions of the society. With this change, individual and group potentials were able to increase and deepen. Living conditions improved and travel increased; religion, education and government were made possible. Ultimately, man discovered that without leaving home he could travel to the farthest regions of

---

[1]See Ernst Cassirer, *An Essay on Man,* (New Haven, Conn.: Yale University Press, 1944), Chapters II and VIII.

space, share the experiences of those who journey around the world, explore the innermost secrets of the atom and reach across the centuries to share the thoughts of past leaders of our civilization. And, further, he could relive these experiences anytime he chose to do so.

The degree to which man can transcend his inherent limitations of space and time is, as mentioned earlier, directly dependent upon the nature of his particular system of symbolization.[2] As noted earlier, the number and functional complexity of the symbols reveal the nature, scope, direction and strength of past interactions experienced by members of the society using the system. These record, also, the value system of that society, for they preserve concepts and objects which have been considered important as they preserve and reflect their degree of importance. The Greeks have three words for *love,* most societies have only one. The Eskimo, it is said, has at least a half dozen words for *snow,* while many of the Polynesian tribes have none. Most societies can refer to the concept of *history* by using any one of several words; the Trobriander tribe does not have one. The nature of the system is such that no speech is *truly* personal. The tribal vocabulary, the rules of grammar and the common experiences of group members combine to guide the individual's speech in a highly predictable fashion. Any use of conventional symbols carries the mark of previous order and organization which must always play its role — no matter how incidental. To know a particular system of symbolization, therefore, is to know the culture of the people who created the system. To know a system of sounds is to be able to detect within its aural anatomy, the reflections of both the lights and shadows of past centuries.

But with all of its marvels, as with all things human, the process of symbolization carries within itself the seeds of its own destruction. As man began to appreciate the true value of release from the prison of his internal and external environments, he began to immortalize his liberator — the symbol. Easily misled by his desire to seek a cause for every effect, man soon believed that the symbol was, *in fact,* the very thing or function it represented. Soon, it was easy to believe that by controlling the symbol he controlled the thing itself. He believed that mere articulation of the symbol was synonymous with exerting definite and dramatic control over the person, place or function. So, even God could be controlled (note the Commandment "Thou shalt not take the name of the Lord, thy God, in vain"); that by changing the symbols for it an unpleasant experience or a threatening force could be made less unpleasant or less threatening (note the substitution of "passed away"

---

[2]*Ibid.,* pp. 29-35, 130-136.

for "died" and "conflict" for "war"); that by assuming a title, one could assume the qualities associated with that title (note such nicknames as "Duke" or "Tiger" or "Killer"). Such beliefs exist today. Because of this belief in the power of words, most societies — even in the age of missiles — still use oaths, blessings, curses, prayers, treaties and the like.

This is not to say that man has consistently ignored the relationship between the symbol and what it represents. During Biblical times, Hebrew scholars tried to describe the nature and scope of this connection. The early Greeks pondered the problem as well. And medieval scholars gave their concern dramatic proportions by holding laborious debates over the nature of this relationship. Some declared that not only were the symbol and the referent inseparable but that the very process of thinking was made possible only by the ability to articulate symbols. So strongly did some medievalists believe this, that the habit of silent reading was discouraged in many schools and monasteries. Other medieval scholars were inclined to consider symbols as arbitrary, conventionalized patterns that were constantly subject to change. They reasoned that since every symbol is a convention or a commonly agreed upon substitute for something else, and since these agreements vary from society to society, no natural bond is in evidence. It is this school of thought which identifies the semantist's approach to oral communication today.

This approach argues that within any given society the original agreements vary as the symbols are used by different individuals who are removed in time, space or maturity from the *original act* of agreement. This distance of time and space, in addition to adding the differences of custom, manner, ideals and general experiences which inevitably develop, tends to lessen the degree of conscious involvement. It is observed in the present day citizen who wishes to talk about alchemy or jousting or voodoo. It is epitomized by the modern student entering a building named for a distinguished person. To the student, it is just a name (which he often mispronounces) attached to a building which he uses impersonally; to the donors, it is a memory which is relived and stimulated with each encounter. Thus, every communicator must realize that the bond between symbols and objects changes from culture to culture and within cultures, changes occur from time to time and from speaker to speaker. *All that is really required is that symbols are used in accordance with certain traditions and, when they are not, both speaker and listener be made aware of the manner in which they are being used.*

The traditions surrounding every society's system of symbolization allow for both social needs and individual preferences. While the degree to which this is allowed varies from society to society, most all groups expect social usage to be in occasional competition with private usage. And the more the communicators move away from a concern with the concrete and simple phenomena in the surroundings, the more definite becomes the competition. As attention turns to such functions as relationships, feelings, desires and moods instead of objects ("love" instead of "you") the more difficult it becomes to use symbols correctly. In other words, while the number and nature of symbols used by two individuals in a given culture can be objectively recorded, the *actual meaning* cannot. Why not?

To understand another human being's communicative efforts, one must seek to understand his understanding of the social concept — the common denominator permitting speaker-listener or writer-reader interaction. Some speakers, having lived widely and experienced deeply, realize the symbols of society permit and even encourage ambiguity; other speakers do not. Certain communicators are aware of the fact that some symbols *create* a concept while others merely *represent* one (as in poetic communication, for example). Other speakers realize that one symbol may act in both capacities and, many times, most symbols do. Many look upon social meanings as static representations of traditional thoughts, passions and actions; and move to rebel against them. As a definite blow against convention, tradition or authority, many subgroups within a society devise their own special meanings for common symbols (note the current meanings of *camp, tough, fuzz, stud,* and so forth). During moments of military occupation, many times special meanings are constructed for common symbols in order to insure secrecy and to deal a silent blow against the convention of the moment. Thus, pinpointing even the more objective and standardized meanings of the symbols employed by a speaker in any given situation is a difficult but necessary undertaking.

Moreover, to understand another man's attempt at communication, one must understand the nature, scope and strength of his *private interpretation* of the social meaning attached to the symbols he employs. As noted earlier, every experience of modern man — imbedded as it is in symbolic activity — serves to modify his stockpile of traditional reactions to the symbols he uses in having and sharing these experiences. A man who has experienced the excruciating and continual stabs of osteomyelitis for twenty years, interprets the word *pain* (both in speaking and hearing it) quite differently than a person who has felt nothing worse than a skinned knee. Since man continues to have experiences from the cradle to the grave, possibilities for a constant and continuing modification of personal or subjective meanings increase rather than decrease. Is it any wonder that misunderstandings are a very large part of man's daily communication?

But his knowledge and use of the symbols of his accepted language account for only part of his confused and misunderstood attempts at communication. Since these same symbols may be written as well as spoken, since each form has its peculiar strengths and weaknesses, any indiscriminate use compounds the possibilities of error and inefficiency. In other words, no amount of understanding regarding the nature of symbolization will replace the need for additional knowledge of the nature of communication of which the use of symbols is but one part. More specifically, the efficient communicator must have an understanding of the various factors — in addition to proper use of symbols — which make up this basic and complex human act. He must appreciate the existence of two major forms of communication for which he is responsible and from which others gain impressions of his knowledge, appreciations and understandings; he is aware of the existence of both the shadow and substance of his communication; he recognizes that he communicates nonverbally as well as verbally.

NONVERBAL COMMUNICATION

Nonverbal communication consists of those aspects of human behavior which convey messages regardless of the lack of recognized symbols such as words, lights, numbers, and the like. Many times, in spite of the speaker-writer, thoughts and feelings are conveyed which are completely different from those intended by the speaker or transmitted by the words. As an example, the physical surroundings generally associated with a person tend — rightly or wrongly — to reveal something of his sense of values regarding himself, his fellows and his organization. "Show me," says an old European adage, "where, when and how a man works and I will tell you how tall, wide and deep his values are." While we may decry the fact, a man is judged by the office he keeps, the car he drives, the home he lives in. Other things being equal, a teacher with a neat, accessible and well-organized office or classroom will tend to be accepted more often than one who demonstrates the opposite.

In the same vein, communicators who exhibit some care about the type of communicative effort they construct present a *metamessage*, or a "superior," message which often helps to make their experience a successful one. With some topics, for some people, in certain places, the oral mode of communication is much more successful than the written. In fact, in some instances, selection of the inappropriate type or mode of communication is tantamount to failure. A written citation of offenses may be indispensable to the dismissal of an employee on civil service or tenure provisions, but would be considered pompous and insensitive if delivered daily. For regular face to face interaction, the average person expects — and should receive — oral communication. For the more formal, the more routinized and the more permanent, written communication is both desirable and necessary. Whenever these expectations are not met, whenever the type of communication is different enough (for the audience, time, place and occasion) to call attention to itself, efficiency is minimized if not precluded.

But even after the more appropriate type of communication is selected, various nonverbal factors play a part in determining the success or failure of the effort. When writing, for instance, the choice of *material* conveys as much of a message as the words themselves. The word of God came to Moses written in stone, to Joseph Smith of the Mormons on golden tablets and to other prophets and oracles in media which the people understood. Notice, in our own time, the different reactions to slick magazines, pulp pamphlets, contracts written on tissue paper, wedding announcements sent out on paper napkins, notices written on a sheet torn from a loose-leaf notebook and so forth. In written efforts, along with the material employed, the communicator constructs meta-messages by his selection of the recording agent. Again, one need not elaborate upon the well-known traditions of covenants written in blood, the insistence upon ink for legal pacts, the reactions against personal letters written in pencil or crayons and the persuasion of a formally printed card or program or textbook as opposed to those which are typewritten or mimeographed. Finally, quite apart from the message shaped by the written words, the communicator "speaks" through his handwriting. While the average reader-listener is not enough of an expert in such subtleties to attempt a psychoanalysis, he is nevertheless enough of a sensitive human to be affected by illegible chicken scratches which pass for writing. He is equally affected by handwriting which strives to be too elegant, which calls attention to itself because of its studied attempts at embellishment. All this added to words which are scribbled, crowded and disconnected leads the communicant to give less attention to the message.

In like manner, if the communicator selects the oral mode of interaction, he must be aware of certain nonverbal factors which help determine his success or failure in any given situation. The most influential factors associated with oral communication are those which arise from the speaker's *use and misuse of his body* during the interaction. While the consideration of bodily action will be explained more fully in a later chapter, it must be said in passing that such nonverbal clues as taps, pats, slaps, handshakes, pointing, frowning and winking carry more meaning — at times — than the formal message; at other times, they reinforce the meaning of the message; at all times, they emit meaning which is used by the sensitive listener in evaluating the entire communication.

Both written and oral modes of communication are helped or hindered by the metamessages delivered by the *time* element. As shall be explained more in detail in the chapter on listener participation, the communicant is impressed (correctly or incorrectly) by how long the communicator allows for his communication, when he attempts his communication (day, night, morning, between other events and the like), and in what order he presents his material and all similar matters involving the time element.

VERBAL COMMUNICATION

Throughout man's long and dynamic evolution, no revolution or war or natural calamity has ever reduced the importance of his verbal communication. If anything, these have served to dramatize its significance in every phase of his activity as they have served to demonstrate the indispensable role played by the oral form. While writing performs a prominent part of shaping and preserving man's heritage, while it serves as an important sign of the educated person, its indispensability cannot begin to compete with that of speaking. It is conceivable that man can go about in this world without having to read or write (over one-half of the world's population still does), but it is impossible to conceive of any society of man which is without spoken forms. Of the approximately three thousand languages in the world today, only about 25% have written forms but 100% have oral forms. One can judge the civilization of man by the degree to which he converses. To the aborigines of Australia as well as the scholar in France, to the child in Lapland as well as the judge in Seattle, the oral mode of communication is the most important tool for personal development and social interaction. Thus, the focus of this book is the oral mode.

On September 20, 1954 during convocation ceremonies at Brown University, President A. Whitney Griswold of Yale University observed that this was a tongue-tied democracy which had all but lost the will and the skill to speak.[a] Assuming that this is an accurate appraisal of America's condition, how does one account for it? Does the fault lie with a lethargic public or with inept professionals? As in most cases,

---

[a]A. Whitney Griswold, "This Tongue-Tied Democracy," *Vital Speeches* 21 (November 1, 1954), p. 829.

the truth probably rests somewhere in between these extremes. Without doubt, past habits of some inept professionals have encouraged a lethargic public; conversely, a public interested more in performance than principle, more in quantity than quality has given encouragement to the ever-present charlatan. As a consequence, the study of oral communication (now as at other times throughout its long history) has been conceived by many to be a study of the trivial, little more than a concentration upon style or the development of a cultured accent which is taken as the *sine qua non* of the Good Life. But even during periods of apparent decay, the serious study of oral communication has never ceased to develop wholesomely.

Today, in the midst of the decadence described by President Griswold, the study of speech with all of its ramifications is a flourishing pursuit — flourishing even by the standards of our inflationary age. There are now chairs and assistantships for speech in almost every large American university, public and private clinics for speech and hearing therapy, active national and regional professional societies, at least a dozen professional journals devoted to general and special problems in the field and, above all, programs of research which promise to furnish a greater understanding of the intricacies of this most human form of communication.

Such research concerns itself with both the abnormal and normal aspects of oral communication. In the area of the abnormal, investigators are seeking, among other things, to discover significant relationships between certain environmental factors and a child's tendency to stutter, between types of occupation and special forms of deafness, between prescribed methods of speech therapy and successful restoration of speech to persons deprived of the power through injury or disease. In the area of the normal, researchers are trying to determine whether women are more susceptible to certain forms of persuasion than are their male counterparts, whether presentations airing one side of an argument are more influential than those which offer two, whether certain personality traits are more closely correlated with effective group leadership than are certain others, whether definite relationships exist among socio-political conditions and the dominant speech theory of any given period, and so on. Thus, in many ways and in varied areas, professionals in the field of oral communication are exploring the endless problems associated with the process which enables *man to commune with man*, and more — which provides *the only true intimacy, the merger of soul with soul.*

This unique process is best characterized by a paradox which is implied in the previous statement, namely: "Man can communicate only what he has in common with other men, but that each communication is properly individual." While, as a highly complex process, it is rooted in the conventions of symbolization (with standard symbols *and* standard experiences) it is also shaped by the peculiarities of specific people, specific places, and definite times. While it is true that every normal member of a society draws from a common reservoir of symbols, experiences and values, the application of them is determined by individual interpretation. Whether it be employed by the Swahili natives of Africa, the nomadic Eskimos of the frozen north or former presidents of the United States, whether it is applied in law courts, in Congress, in church, school or home, the process of speech inevitably includes individual idiosyncracies of *attitude, thought, bodily action, voice* and *language*. And, according to how these are proportionally modified as they become more or less integrated with the others, the total act of speech (the total attempt at oral communication) will become either a success or a failure. (See Figure 1.)

Of all these factors which help to determine the nature of an individual act of oral communication, least appreciated are the *attitudes* of the persons involved. For purposes of this discussion, attitudes shall be conceived of as learned and relatively stable tendencies to respond in predetermined fashion to certain objects or situations. The attitudes held by each person develop out of his experiences and are shaped particularly by social interaction. With but a moment's reflection most of us can recall many personal attitudes that reflect time, place and status of birth, early schooling, religious training, as well as other social experiences. With but a moment more, we realize these same attitudes were shaped during situations or experiences especially dominated by oral communication. No group of attitudes evidences a closer bond with the process of oral communication than those which each person forms about the "self." In like manner, few groups of attitudes demonstrate a more positive effect upon individual communicative prowess than those of self. Most psychologists and philosophers appear to agree with George Mead's observation that the self concept is based upon the concepts others have manifested towards us which, in turn, help to determine our behavior patterns.[4] For example, a child knows that he is good or bad as a result of what he is told by parents, teachers and friends; a young lady comes to know herself as pleasant, charming and attractive when others react by telling her so; a business man considers himself successful, friendly and capable because the verbal (and non-

---

[4]George Mead, *Mind, Self and Society* (Chicago: University of Chicago Press, 1934), pp. 135-36.

verbal) reactions of others have helped him shape such conclusions. And so it goes.

It is this same phenomenon which underlies the problem of stage fright. Largely due to earlier experiences in which one sees himself or others suffer from incompetence, certain exaggerated reaction patterns develop regarding oral communication situations. There arises an over-awareness of the self, an abnormal concern with the disintegrative processes and an inability to engage in effective communication. While it is true that most individuals advance from adolescence to old age with a lack of introspection, it does not necessarily follow that all persons are qualified to engage in such activity, nor that all persons will profit from it. There is much to be said for the view that "soul-searching" could encourage a distorted view of the searcher, the world and life generally.

Properly analyzed, the symptoms of stage fright — perspiring hands, "cotton mouth," trembling knees and "butterfly" stomach — are seen to be but normal physiological reactions to an apparent threatening situation. Without such reactions, one would be either unconscious or dead. These are the same symptoms, essentially, which occur whenever one faces a situation which harbors real or imagined opportunities for punishment or failure: athletic contests, social events, intellectual competition and the like. History records that famous speakers, whatever their proficiency, have always experienced such symptoms. The essential difference between the novice and the professional is that the latter channels the energy behind such symptoms into his talk, while the novice permits this same energy to impede his attempts. The efficient communicator recognizes these symptoms as normal and feels free to engage in bodily action which is appropriate and which acts as a release for his pent-up energy.

In each of the simplified instances just cited, the effects of such attitudes upon one's ability to communicate are obvious. The degree of emotional adjustment and mental objectivity is reflected in the organization of thoughts, choice of words, tone of voice, bodily actions and the like. So it is with attitudes regarding others.

Beyond few obvious factors, to know that an individual is an American or a Frenchman or a German is not enough to enable anyone to say what his attitudes are towards specific situations or, more particularly, towards people. However, exposed to a series of speaking performances by this same individual, one would be able to make some valid judgments concerning these same attitudes. Basic *awareness, respect, sensitivity, flexibility* and *understanding* tend to reveal themselves through one or all of the interrelated aspects of speech. Perhaps here more than anywhere else are revealed the important ethical standards which bind an individual to his society. Here, more than anywhere else, the individual defines his goals, ambitions, and responsibilities; here, in his attitudes towards others, either rests the driving force that could reduce civilization to the level of the ants, the lizards, and the snakes or move it forward to greater gains and more impressive glories.

In truth it would appear that the perennial problems of civilization — Grecian difficulties epitomized by Demosthenes, Roman tribulations voiced by Cicero, medieval problems phrased by Dante, Renaissance confusions emphasized by Machiavelli and Galileo and modern crises crystallized by Hitler, Stalin, or McCarthy — are not scientific or technological; rather they are ethical problems of persuasion; they are problems created by the attitudes of man towards man, and perpetrated by the unethical use of the basic process of communication: speech.[5] Is it not obvious that among other things one's attitudes toward others would dictate his selection, organization and presentation of the facts of any given case? Is it not patent that proper attitudes towards others such as awareness, respect, sensitivity, flexibility and understanding furnish the internal gyroscope which permits the process of speech to be used mainly for *communal* rather than *individual* gain? Is it not easily discerned, as shown in Figure 2, that anyone interested in improving his ability to communicate orally must be as intimately concerned with his attitudes as he is with his ability to articulate the symbols of the language?

A second major aspect of this important and complicated process of speech is *thought*. Whatever the precise relationship between *thought* and *speech*, certain it is that good, effective speech includes all aspects of thought ranging from signal responses to reflective judgments. Various speaking forms from conversation through formal debate — if they are to be effective — must include the basic processes of joining, modifying or diminishing the materials furnished to us by our senses. In terms of perceptions, for example, the speaker must be aware of the speaking situation itself; he must manifest the ability to identify a *need* for communication (this is part of the difficulty outlined by Dr. Griswold in his claim that this is a tongue-tied democracy); he must also be able to discriminate among the various elements of the situation: the nature of the listener, the time, the place, the nature of the subject, and so on.

In addition to basic realizations, the speaker must be capable of certain interpretations. Among other things, he must have effective

<hr />

[5] Richard McKeon, *Thought, Action and Passion* (Chicago: University of Chicago Press, 1954), p. 4ff. See also William H. White, Jr., *Individualism Old and New* (New York: Menton, Balch, 1930) pp. 87-88.

recall and the capacity to relate bits of knowledge; he must, in many instances, make instantaneous (and valid) inferences, exercise good judgment and be capable of lucid, rewarding imagination. He must be accomplished in all these, and still more, for the ultimate end of these perceptions and interpretations is to order and arrange the raw material so that effective communication can be achieved.

This phase of ordering and arranging includes an *external* as well as an *internal* division. External ordering refers to the organization and/or adjustment of certain relations between speaker and listener (perhaps the listener is predisposed to reject whatever this speaker offers), between message and listener (perhaps the ideas are too difficult and demand greater elaboration for this particular audience), between message, time and place (perhaps the ideas are too controversial or too difficult to be presented completely at this time and in this place) and so forth. External ordering has to do with the organization of the phases of a communicative situation over and above the message itself; it has to do with the *plan of the whole*. Internal ordering concerns itself with the organization of the specific ideas which constitute the message. It is here that the speaker (either prior to the actual speaking event or during it) decides the precise sequence in which his ideas will be uttered; it is here that he determines the relative importance of his ideas, matters of cumulation and climax, points of elaboration and the like. The phases of thought included in the process of speech, therefore, consist of discovering, noting, interpreting and ordering bits of knowledge immediately applicable to any given speech situation. These phases will be analyzed more thoroughly at another point in this work.

A third major aspect of the speaking process is *bodily action*. This refers to the patterns of activity which most people think of when hearing the word *delivery* as applied to speech. As with Demosthenes, most people would cite this phase of the entire process as being the most important. Unlike Demosthenes, however, contemporary champions of delivery would be thinking solely of gesture and movement. Properly, bodily action in speech, that is, the physical action which forms a specific part of every speaking occasion, consists of three phases: (1) the sensory phase or the reception of stimuli from the surrounding environment (the operation of the senses of audition, vision, touch, kinesthesis); (2) the associative phase or the integration of various neural activities which usually takes place in the cerebral cortex, but which may include such lower parts of the brain as the cerebellum; (3) the effective phase or the activity or completion phase which demands the action of muscles and glands. The most obvious aspect of this last phase is, as has already been mentioned, gesture or movement. And perhaps because of its obvious nature, it is this part which has blossomed forth to a point where it is easily confused with the whole. True, awkward and irrelevant movements have often served to confuse, indeed, to belie the meaning of oral symbols used by a speaker; however, it does not follow — as some of the older elocutionists would have us believe — that most effective communication will come with improvement in and emphasis on gesture. As a supplement and to the clarifying agent other aspects of the total process, normal gestures characteristic of the individual furnish positive aid to all speakers. Equally important, though less frequently considered, is the role played by covert muscular activity like the neuro-muscular activity related to breathing, posture and movement.

Directly dependent upon bodily action is *voice*, the fourth major aspect of the total process of speech. Within the human species, voice is produced as a result of the integration of four major activities. The first of these is breathing, the process of respiration which provides the force for human voice. Unlike the respiration which helps to sustain life, breathing for speech includes inspiration and controlled expiration. The second of these major activities which produces voice is phonation, the oscillating action of the vocal folds resulting from the passage of the breath stream upon expiration. The third activity involved in human voice production is resonance, amplification and reinforcement of sound waves in the cavities and occasionally in the solid structures of the upper body. After respiration, phonation and resonance have produced a steady stream of sound, articulation, the fourth activity, produces the distinctive sounds characteristic of particular culture. The tongue, lips, teeth, jaw and palate act as modifying agents which shape the resonators and help form the various consonants and vowels peculiar to each language.

Through the ages — in one form or another — people have believed that *voice reveals personality.* "Let me hear his voice," they say, "and I will tell you what kind of man he is." While the statement is, of course, exaggerated, it is nevertheless true that people *do* use voice as an indicator of personality and with some justification. The pitch, volume, quality and rate of an individual's voice do vary during changes in temperament and, from the layman's point of view, certain vocal patterns are characteristic of certain temperaments. (Chapter 6 will deal with voice more extensively.)

In addition to attitude, thought, bodily action and voice, the fifth and final process of speech is *language.* And this, it will be recalled, is where the discussion began with the matter of symbolization. As used in speech, symbolization means spoken sounds or combinations of sounds which form words. The individual speaker's symbolic prowess is partially revealed by his diction (choice of words) and his composition. Diction involves use of personal vocabularies; composition involves a regard for matters of grammar and style. Since habits of style change and since style should reflect an adjustment to the needs of the audience and the occasion, effective speakers continually work to develop a facility of varied styles. This, too, will be discussed more fully later.

SUMMARY

The previous thoughts have been focused on man's system of symbolization and the involvement of that system in both nonverbal and verbal communication. This ability of man to transform his experiences into ideas and in turn into symbols which he can manipulate with purpose and effectiveness is his sole liberating agent. The artificial bond between symbol and meaning, if not evaluated properly, leads him into confusions and misunderstandings which may be as tragic as they are comical. Effective communicators exercise care in defining a common meaning between themselves and their listener-readers. Moreover, the careful communicator realizes that he transmits his intended message in addition to several metamessages which he may not intend.

Verbal communication, whether written or oral, is man's most common tool for social interaction. The most important of the two verbal modes, the oral, also proves to be the most complicated. It involves social traditions and experiences which are shaped and interpreted before they are offered as public utterances. When they are, it is as a result of the co-ordination of the speaker's attitudes, thoughts, bodily action, voice, and language.

PRACTICAL REMINDERS

Propositions

1. Man's thoughts are shaped by the nature of the language he uses in conceiving and expressing them.

2. Man draws from and contributes to society's reservoir of traditions every time he seeks to communicate.

3. Man communicates with man by verbal and nonverbal means and usually combines these in every communicative act.

4. Oral communication is a complex and dynamic tool useful in the development of both the individual and his society.

Exercises

1. With some friends, try to establish an extended communication for a period of fifteen minutes *without using* speech, writing or formalized pantomime. At the conclusion of the period, compare reactions *before* messages are compared.

2. List as many occupations as possible which *do not* require a direct or indirect dependence upon oral communication for their creation, maintenance or development.

Readings

Black, Max (ed.), *The Importance of Language*, Englewood Cliffs, N. J.: Prentice-Hall, Inc., 1962.

Cassirer, Ernst, *Language and Myth*, New York: Harper and Bros., 1946.

Rahskopf, Horace G., *Basic Speech Improvement*, New York: Harper & Row, Publishers, 1965.

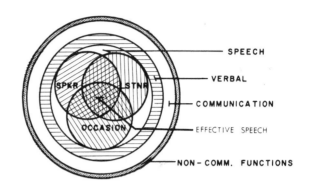

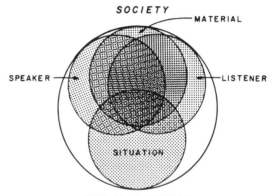

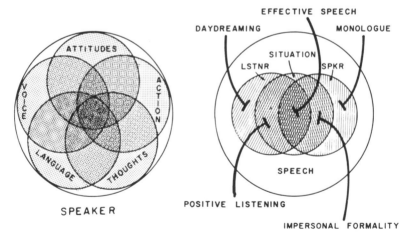

FIGURE 1

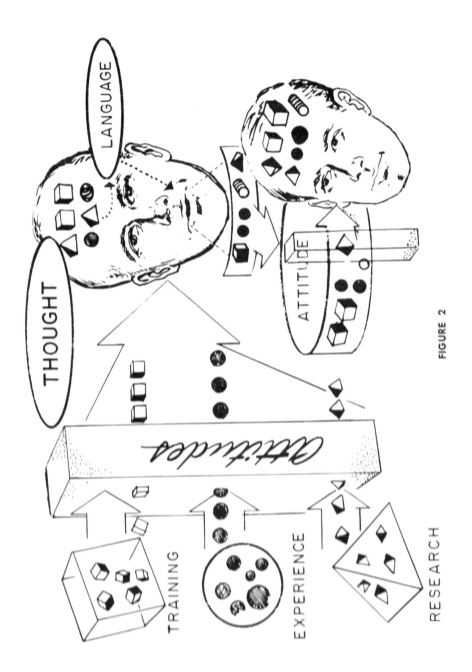

LANGUAGE

THOUGHT

ATTITUDE

Attitudes

TRAINING

EXPERIENCE

RESEARCH

FIGURE 2

19

Chapter 2

PRINCIPLES OF EFFECTIVE ORAL COMMUNICATION

The task of the competent oral communicator is to understand the nature of communication so he may appreciate the rationale for any principles which he applies in the concrete situation.

As with all aspects of social behavior, oral communication can never be dissected and stratified enough to permit the infallible control and prediction common to some physical sciences. Nevertheless, as a consequence of more regularized and controlled observations, this important act of man is understood enough to permit the formulation of various principles which get him beyond the sporadic successes occasioned by his "common-sense knowledge." As the physical and social worlds become more and more complicated and complex, the "universals" derived from rule of thumb reasoning must be replaced by principles which will prove successful in most specific instances of interaction.

In the twenty-five hundred year history of the discipline of speech in Western civilization, various principles have been articulated from time to time and country to country. Each attempt was a step toward better understanding and, through it, greater effectiveness. Through the years, tested in the crucible of demanding societies, many specific rules have been preserved and transmitted to the people of this age. However, broader principles, unlike the specific rules mentioned in the preceding, have not been transmitted from age to age and society to society. Where they exist, they reflect the specific needs and values of the society which shaped them and thereby work to preserve these same needs and values. Currently, the strong democratic emphasis reflected in most of the Western world seems to argue for the development of a set of principles for oral communication which reflect that emphasis. The principles which follow represent an attempt to describe (and prescribe) effective oral communication within a society which is democratic in environment.

PRINCIPLE A

In its effective state, oral communication is organized, meaningful and selectively particular.

The principle observes the characteristic paradox mentioned in Chapter 1: Man can communicate only that which he shares in common with other men but each communication must be individual and particular. Despite its roots in social agreements and its characteristic of being a public phenomenon (even during the moments of conversations with oneself), oral communication is always individual, personal and private. Both speaker and listener react by their own unique interpretations of the verbal and nonverbal aspects of speech. Whatever the nature of these interpretations, they always reflect the individual's desire for order and meaning. If what he hears and sees is not ordered and clear, the listener will either reject it or instill order and meaning to fit his personal needs. Thus, the sports-minded child learning the Lord's Prayer without the benefit of society's meaning and with minimal knowledge of its language might well recite: "Our Father who got in heaven, allowed the tie game." He might say *sparrow grass* for *asparagus* or *dandy lions* for *dandelions*. The immigrant from Mexico hearing the Star-Spangled Banner for the first time, could easily repeat the first words as "Jose can you see"; or say *Lake Champagne* for *Lake Champlain*. The uneducated status-minded auditor can easily (and intentionally) be misled by speakers who, known for their opposition to education, ask: "Do you know that students are allowed to *matriculate* at Podunk University? That professors force students to show their *theses* before they are allowed to graduate? That male students are allowed to have *discourses* with females?

Realizing this, the competent speaker makes certain that his entire communicative adventure is ordered, developed and maintained in such fashion as to permit his meanings to fill the dominant needs of the listener. To do so, of course, the successful oral communicator maintains a constant appreciation for the role of the listener as an influential factor in prescribing the nature, scope, speed and direction of speech efforts. And he finds this to be especially true when the listener interprets situations as confusing, ambiguous, threatening or otherwise unpleasant.

In similar fashion, the sensitive speaker acknowleges the influence of this tendency to organize and inject meaning when, with the proper audience, time and place, he shouts *ten-hut* instead of *attention*; answers a question with a long, fixed stare instead of words; overlooks the use of a wrong word in a question phrased by a foreigner; or pauses purposefully and responds to a heated and rapid challenge with slow, well-modulated and carefully chosen words.

PRINCIPLE B

The dynamics of oral communication result from the psycho-physical aspects of the immediate environment.

Unlike its written counterpart, oral communication can only be revealed in an "unfolding" process which is within the control of the individual speaker. No one can ascertain with certainty precisely what direction and color the speaker's thoughts will take until he releases them — and this includes the speaker himself, in many instances. This very act of unfolding contains within it the privilege and the *responsibility of modification, of adaptation to the changing needs of the speaker, listener or occasion.* And it is this very flexibility which makes the speech adventure unique and wonderful. As the product of a crisis, a loss of equilibrium between the inner and the outer environments of the speaker-listener complex, it reflects the changes occurring within as well as *between* individuals. The degree of this imbalance varies with the factors involved in each specific situation; it may range from that created by the presence of another who does not fully understand, to that created by one who is definitely opposed. The attempt to adjust the balance, to re-establish what is termed homeostasis in medical psychology,[1] is the continuing goal of all speakers and the occasional achievement of some. This is precisely why the essence of good speech and good speakers is *flexibility;* this is precisely why such things as "canned" speeches (or speakers) are both a travesty and a farce;[2] this is precisely why "ghost-written" speeches cannot possibly be as effective as those conceived, delivered and *modified in the process of delivery by the speaker.*

Toward this end, the competent communicator recognizes that, as a viable art form, good communication manifests a subtle balance between content and form. Because oral communication is not a science, there is no way of knowing the precise degree of emphasis to be exercised by either the content or the form. Only the mind of a sensitive and intelligent man can create the effective proportion which can contribute more than either offers singly. In any given situation, for example, the idea may well be eclipsed by the form — and for valid

---

[1] G. K. Yacorzynski, *Medical Psychology* (New York: The Ronald Press Company, 1951), p. 23.

[2] Note the unbelievable news item in *The Wall Street Journal*, September 8, 1966, p. 1 which announces the availability of a teaching machine designed to produce "instant orators."

reasons. Someone seeking to overcome the charge of being a "shoddy thinker" may well highlight the form in order to achieve his goal. The parent attempting to demonstrate good thought to his child, the lawyer arguing a case before a superior court, the researcher presenting his results before a professional society each might choose to structuralize his communication in this fashion. This is not to say such an imbalance, however slight, ought to be the standard. It is to say there are instances when the presence of form should be made more obvious in view of the final goal; that, conversely, there may be instances where the presence of other than a very loose and vague form would result in the annihilation or rejection of the idea.[3] In the final analysis, the sensitive speaker notes that the precise balance between form and idea is determined by the dynamics of the immediate situation, but in any case, good communication most generally reveals the strength of a real, albeit unobtrusive form. The absence of such an appreciation is readily evident in the actions of an overzealous and poorly educated debater who must always discuss in terms of stock issues, definitions and phrases; in the speaking habits of the dedicated but misguided teacher who must always employ the Socratic method in his daily interactions; in the behavior of the well-intended executive whose communicative efforts always reflect the latest fad in human relations.

PRINCIPLE C

The proper concern of the oral communicator in any given act of communication is the satisfaction of his responsibility as a social organism.

Oral communication, as a communion among humans, is always a compromise between the intentions of the speaker and the expectations of the listener. But more than this, it is first an act of compromise between personal needs and social requirements. As has already been observed, this wonderful and dynamic activity serves both the individual and his society by acting as the tool for the development of both. At any one time, therefore, a conflict often exists over which of the two ends shall dominate during that venture; at other times, a constantly shifting role is assumed so that each goal is partially fulfilled. As a parent, for example, one usually strives to maintain the superiority of the social purpose in his communications with his children. However, as a human being with personal needs of his own, the parent occasionally engages in communication which is more an expression than a com-

---

[3]Saint Augustine, *On Christian Doctrine*, translated by D. W. Robertson, Jr. (New York: The Liberal Arts Press, 1958), p. 37.

munion, more a release for pent-up frustrations than an exercise in guiding the concepts being developed by his offspring. And properly so, for no one can be perennially and exclusively concerned with his social obligations during every act of communication. Even if possible, it ought to be discouraged since it stifles the development of that individual and, thereby, reduces his value in future actions. In a word, the oral communicator's first responsibility as a social organism is the proper development of himself through the maintenance of a regular and fluid mobility between his internal and external environments.[4]

In terms of his personal needs, the sensitive speaker is aware of his need for constant contact with his two worlds (inner and outer) and his need to maintain a bridge between them. He notes, also, that his ability to speak helps him to locate and define his doubts, confusions, feelings and moods for himself even before he is interested in conveying them to others. Is there anyone in contemporary society who has grown to maturity without the experience of speaking *with* and *to* himself?[5] Can there be those who, *in the process of describing a concept to others,* have never come to see it more clearly themselves? Every act of oral communication is a creative act in that it requires the speaker to reach into the general mass of thoughts or feelings which he stores inside of him (and to which he adds regularly), to identify one, give it the best shape possible from those available in the language he is using at the moment, and then try to color, stretch, smooth, scratch and fluff it in such a way as to make it recognized and appreciated by a particular listener. In developing the formless into viable shapes, the individual changes his own storehouse of experiences and thus he changes himself, for it is bits of himself which are contained in his every act of communication — from the breath expended to the thoughts conceived. In truth, the sensitive speaker can say:

> I am pressed between the cutting edges
> of my own teeth,
> Tossed by the movements of my tongue,
> Shaped by the action of my cheeks,
> Bathed in the sound of my own throat,
> Lost in the shadowy regions of my own mind.

For him, particularly, speech offers creation and distinction; it provides continuity to his individual nature and furnishes the means for

---

[4]See Carl R. Rogers, "Communication: Its Blocking and Its Facilitation," *Northwestern University Information* 20 (April 21, 1952), pp. 9-15.

[5]Man has now discovered this process to be indispensable to the successful development and performance of complicated computers. See John Pfeiffer, "Machines That Man Can Talk With," *Fortune* (May, 1964), pp. 2-8.

transporting himself from the depths of introspection to the heights of social communion. It is, in the final analysis, the only true image of his naked, mercurial and personal being.

In terms of his social responsibility, the conscientious speaker reveals his indebtedness to the society of which he is a part by careful, discrete and meaningful use of his power to affect the life of another. Just as speech proves important in his own continuing development, it proves necessary to the life and growth of the speaker's auditors. As shall be seen in Chapters 7 and 8, the oral communicator claims the right, however temporary, to shape and direct the life of another human being. As a parent, teacher, friend or even a stranger, the speaker prescribes exactly how the next few moments of another person's life are to be spent. By asking a question, responding to one or purposely failing to do either, the speaker contributes or detracts from the maturation of the auditor. By clarifying alternatives, defining a universal mood, reinterpreting a half-truth or acting as a catalyst who "delivers in rain what he gathers as mist," the oral communicator contributes to the progress of his fellows. The contribution is made by a sensitive human who identifies the need in his fellow beings for sustenance of mind and spirit as well as body. Thus does the communicator champion the "I-Thou" philosophy.[6] He champions the thought that since speech is the revealer of psychological universes, the barometer of internal pressures and the mirror of the soul,[7] the necessary counterpart of the much-defended freedom of speech is the freedom of silence which he must permit his listener.

As a social organism sharing the privileges of society's heritage and exercising a responsibility of contributing to its progress, the serious student of oral communication maintains the moral obligations inherent in all good discourse.[8] These include the obligation to make and act on competent value judgments regarding people and their ideas without engaging in false human relations or callous indifference; to know and act on the difference between a sincere respect for the worth of the individual and an indiscriminate approval of *any* concepts articulated by *any* speakers. In addition, the oral communicator has an obligation which, although less obvious and rarely discussed, is part of his responsibility to return something to society; it is the obligation to foster and preserve the image of speech as a viable and basic mode of human

[6]Martin Buber, *Between Man and Man* (New York: The Macmillan Company, 1948), pp. 175ff.

[7]Harry Overstreet, *The Mature Mind* (New York: W. W. Norton & Company, Inc., 1949), pp. 13-41.

[8]See David Riesman, "Value in Context," *The American Scholar*, (Winter, 1952/53), p. 35.

interaction. This is done best, of course, by using it to create an image and to discourage any use to the contrary.

PRINCIPLE D

The qualities of communication are improved in proportion as the qualities of the communicator are improved.

If anything in the preceding chapters can be said to be a recurring theme, it is that the nature and importance of oral communication requires attention which must be deep and sustained if it is to be improved. One cannot improve it by acquiring a thin veneer of thumbnail jokes, increased vocabulary and refined gestures any more than one can improve his health by dabbing himself with iodine or taking "pep" pills. Nor can it be improved by three-day institutes or two-week seminars. As with matters of health, oral communication requires development in the more basic areas of man's interior self: attitudes toward himself and the world, thought patterns enabling him to shape those attitudes, knowledge furnishing thought, and a language sensitively handled to insure the depth and color necessary for the understanding and acceptance of thought. Intellectual nourishment of this kind will show itself by sound growth from within in much the same fashion as that derived from the physical nourishment taken in by daily meals. The taller, wider and deeper a man is intellectually, the more proficient he is as a communicator.

SUMMARY

With some, speech is an adventure; with others, it is their history. With some, speech is a personal conclusion; with others, it becomes a universal truth. In all, it is a public ordering of private awareness for social interaction, and as man improves his private capacities his public interaction will also improve.

PRACTICAL REMINDERS

Propositions

1. Effective oral communication can never be epitomized by one example which can apply to all people and all ages.

2. The ingredients of every instance of oral communication — speaker, listener, time, place and subject — all play a part in determining the success of the experience.

3. Speakers more interested in self-expression than in self-improvement will rarely become effective.

4. Any standard approaches to effective speaking, from jokes to phrases, hinder the speaker's effectiveness.

Exercises

1. Try to conduct a communication with a friend by responding to his queries or statements only with appropriate proverbs or adages.

2. Again, with a group of friends, arrange for a few to engage in regular and irrelevant responses to whatever is being said by some of the group who have not been forewarned of this exercise. Record their reactions and note how long this is allowed to continue before it is broken off by questions concerning the "strange behavior."

Readings

Frazer, J. G., *The Golden Bough*, New York: The Macmillan Company, 1949.

Krech, David and Crutchfield, Richard, *Theory and Problems of Social Psychology*. New York: McGraw-Hill Co., 1948.

Morris, Charles, *Signs, Language* and *Behavior*, Englewood Cliffs, N. J.: Prentice-Hall, Inc., 1946.

PART II

ORAL COMMUNICATION
Method and Meaning

*Meaning is born
of method*

James O. Sneddon, Photographer
University of Washington *Alumnus*, Spring 1966
Used by permission.

Chapter 3

SKILLS OF THE SPEAKER:
Speaker-Listener Analysis

Among the numerous experts in the field of communication, there are various definitions of the term persuasion. Some argue there is an important and definite distinction between education and persuasion. The thought is that insofar as one deals with information, persuasion does not enter the scene. The major criterion in this point of view is *facts*. Thus, if the material tends to be factual, if the speaker tends to present the facts as they were discovered, the attempt at communication falls into the category of educational or informative communication.

Others believe that in proportion as a speaker selects materials to be given, organizes and develops them to the satisfaction of the audience, matters of persuasion operate.[1] In other words, whenever an individual has his choice limited or prescribed as a consequence of additional information, his decisions are being directed and therefore persuaded. This applies as much to instances in education as it does to occasions peculiar to law courts. In both areas, much is said about presenting only factual material so that the listener can judge for himself. Yet, the time allotted, the procedures followed and the facts selected have already defined the limits of the listener's choice. Further examples are legion whether drawn from areas of business, industry, religion or the various professions. Whenever one man seeks to gather, organize and present materials to another man, matters of persuasion must play a part.

It is in this broader sense of persuasion that philosophers have long described the problems of civilization as being problems of persuasion. Wars are fought not because we lack technology, but because people have failed in their attempts at persuasion. Overpopulation, smoking, vice, carnage on the highways, delinquency and divorce all remain

---

[1]See Harold C. Martin, *The Logic and Rhetoric of Exposition*, (New York: Henry Holt & Company, Inc., 1958), pp. 76ff.

problems as long as failure marks the various attempts to persuade people to alter their behavior. Men work in harmony with each other in matters of religion, education, industry and health as a consequence of successful, persuasive communication. Lack of harmony in each of these areas is an accurate index of unsuccessful attempts at persuasion.

Since the time man first recognized the importance of systematizing his attempts to communicate with other men, he has identified certain elements as basic to the matter of persuasion. These he has identified as the speaker, the message and the occasion, all of which are related so as to produce a desired response in a particular listener. In short, every single act of communication is a definite specialized attempt by a speaker to *persuade a definite specialized listener at a definite specialized time*. At this point, therefore, it seems appropriate to discuss the roles played by speaker and listener.

SPEAKER ANALYSIS

Regardless of the age of the individual, irrespective of his walk of life, he tends to be influenced by the very nature of other people with whom he deals. For most of their young lives, children place their hope and trust in those adults with whom they have frequent and close contact. These, of course, are their parents. As they grow older, the shift in confidence and trust occurs — sometimes completely, sometimes partially — from parents to teachers to friends. In any large social unit from institutions to governments, adults are inclined to believe certain people and to distrust others. *And it is this appeal which*, in the ill-defined areas of communication, *carries much more impact than the arguments themselves*. With but a moment's reflection, we recall from our own experiences that from some people we are inclined to accept the strongest chastisement and from others we are inclined to reject an equally strong compliment. The early Greeks sought to define this reaction in terms of the listener's *integrity, competence* and *good will*.

Integrity

In Chapter 1 mention was made of the ethical standards which bind an individual to his society. On the basis of mutual values, speaker and listener can proceed in their symbolic activity by effecting agreements, making commitments and generally directing the course of many lives. Of the ethical standards alluded to during the earlier discussion, none is more eminent than integrity.

If in the course of prior publicity, or during the presentation of the speech itself, the audience is inclined to question the sincerity or honesty of the speaker, his arguments will be rejected regardless of their value. On the other hand, as we have repeatedly experienced, a speaker conceived by the audience to be honest, sincere and his own man will have his arguments accepted — many times — in spite of an inherent weakness contained within them. However, the greatest force in the creation of an image of integrity is the speech itself. It is as though here, in the presence of the audience, the speaker bares his innermost image. If this image is one of an individual who has read widely, who speaks only of what he firmly believes and who has respect for the most important conventions of his society, his integrity will be established. If, on the other hand, his image is revealed as one who speaks opportunistically, who is inclined to handle ideas and feelings with the obvious mark of a shallow man, his integrity will be questioned. Unfortunately, our social experience is such that we have already recognized categories of men whose integrity is challenged automatically. Surely in describing an individual, you have heard others say he is "just a salesman." The thought here, of course, is that salesmen are inclined to say anything and everything so long as they can achieve their desired end. While this may not be true, the image has been strongly created in our society. Obviously, the easiest way to create the image of integrity is to be a man of integrity. Every listener, from single witnesses to multitudes, would prefer to associate with men in whom the inner man and outer man are one. Particularly in this complex period of human civilization, people are continually disturbed and repelled by those who pretend to be one thing while they are another. The fatigue derived from trying to measure a man by his communication is forcing most people to accept the alternative of simple and complete rejection of those who pose a problem. In these special moments of crises, in these times when actions as well as ideas appear to be so transient and viable, persuasion assumes greater potency. The following principle passed on to us from ancient civilization has not lost its truthfulness through the passage of time: *The good speaker is the good man speaking well.* Even greater force is gathered by the marriage of integrity and competence.

Competence

Rare is the situation where listeners will be persuaded by speakers who show an obvious lack of competence in the material being discussed. Obviously, a lay opinion about the treatment of a certain disease will not carry as much force as the opinion of a qualified medical doctor on the same subject. A talk by a member of the accounting staff arguing for test drillings in a certain area will be less effective than the same talk delivered by a geologist. Such obvious and complete qualification, however, is not always available or possible. The fluid nature of today's society demands that each person assume a variety of roles in the course of daily living. And for each role, however long it endures, we are expected to demonstrate a minimal degree of competence. As a father, husband, friend, schoolboard member, churchgoer, student leader, we are often expected to demonstrate our speaking competence whenever we speak. What value do we place on the comments of a childless father talking about child rearing? Of a bachelor speaking about the ideal marriage? Of a teen-ager about the trials and tribulations of the depression of the early 1930s?

Competence is gained through the wise and regular use of three major avenues of knowledge: *experience, training* and *research.*

Today a popular notion is that experience is the best teacher. This false notion, more often repeated than understood, has led many persons to assume a negative attitude toward training and research. As a consequence, their own efficiency is quite well described by the nature of their past lives. Experience, in fact, is the worst teacher since it gives the test first and the lesson later. Learn by experience, for example, that iodine is poisonous to humans; that one should not stand in front of a turbojet engine when it is turned on; that wet fingers stuck into an electric socket could be fatal. Worse yet, experience is a poor teacher since it offers no controls to guarantee the learning of good habits instead of bad. For this reason, all experience is not necessarily good experience. One may learn by experience to become very good at being very bad.

Training is more efficient since material is learned in shorter time and in better fashion. One may, for example, move from the status of an amateur to civil engineer in approximately four to five years of intensive and directed training. To be sure, a better possibility would be to have a combination of training and experience. Even so, one can become quite rigid in his thinking and stereotyped in his habits if he restricts his endeavors to those learned by training and experience. Unless these two aspects are continuously broadened by regular research (reading, discussions, interviews) they will soon be outdated.

Continuous research is demanded in this age as man finds himself more and more removed from direct experience with his environment and no longer in direct, systematic and sustained contact with the world of nature. As an intelligent citizen he finds it practically impossible to function without a dependence on certain mediators. Even with all of the advantages of jet travel and adequate finances, the average person can hardly travel through all of China, interview the heads of state in Europe, watch the Olympics in Rome or become involved enough in the politics of emerging nations. Nevertheless, he is often required to act — symbolically or in reality — on the basis of information concerning events, places and things, such as those mentioned above, which he has never personally experienced. In truth, the modern citizen's judgments and actions are governed largely by the nature and the efficacy of mediators which stand between him and the various phenomena making up his environment. Throughout the history of mankind certain individuals or groups have seized upon this opportunity and have sought to control others by directing the mediating agents.[2] Thus, the influence of man's nonpersonal sources (books, newspapers, radio, TV, other people, etc.) is profound enough to merit the attention of anyone interested in improving himself and his society.

Without question, the most extensive source of information available to the literate man of the twentieth century is the printed word. So vast is this storehouse of information that no single system of classifying and recording available data exists. Nonetheless, certain more reliable systems have been constructed in the attempt to reduce the complexity of the situation facing the average individual.

To begin with, the interested student of effective oral communication should become familiar with available libraries within his community. This should include, of course, those libraries located in the city, in newspaper plants, in colleges and universities, in smaller public and private schools and in certain federal facilities such as army bases and so forth. Within each library, the student should note the location and special features of the reference rooms, periodical collections, card catalogues, and other particulars.

Reference rooms in most libraries contain such general source materials as dictionaries, encyclopedias (general and special), biographies, government records and so forth. In addition, most of them contain the major indices needed to locate information on specific topics. Among the more common indices of this sort, one should become familiar with *Poole's Index to Periodical Literature* (which records articles published in popular journals before 1900); *Readers' Guide to Periodical Literature* (which records articles published in popular journals after 1900); *International Index to Periodicals* (which records scholarly articles for the professional journals published since early 1900); *The New York Times Index* (which catalogues information published in *The New York Times* newspaper since its first publication; *Cumulative Book Index* (which notes the newest books issued each year). There are, in addition, the

---

[2]Overstreet, *op. cit.*, p. 227.

more specialized indices dealing with particular fields (*Index to Legal Periodical Literature, Education Index, Industrial Arts Index, Index Medicus*) or with particular journals.

After a good exploration of the reference rooms in the nearest libraries, the conscientious citizen should make himself familiar with the periodical collections available to him. During this investigation, he should try to determine the nature, extent and location of the holdings. Many libraries keep two or three of the current issues of a periodical on open shelves and the back issues beneath these same shelves or in some stacks located nearby. In any event, the individual should be aware of the several categories of periodicals. From scholarly and accurate publications such as *American Scholar, Classical Review, Journal of the History of Ideas, Economist, Harper's, Scientific American, Vital Speeches,* and others of this type, one can move to those more popular, less accurate publications which are available on corner newsstands. In making the decision of which periodical to use, one should consider that quarterlies are generally more concerned with accuracy of fact and depth of value than are weeklies, but no periodical is beyond the possibility of having serious error and prejudice. Finally, many libraries classify their newspapers with journals and will probably store them in the same area. Because most newspapers are under serious and continuing pressures to meet the competition, they tend to be less concerned with accuracy than with saleable news. Reporters, copy writers and copy readers and city editors usually work under pressures of speed and drama rather than calm reflection and prolonged investigation. Although some are more reliable, more consistent and less dramatic, the very nature of the industry argues against the probability that newspapers will ever become a major source of trustworthy information. Still, such papers as *The New York Times, The Christian Science Monitor, Washington Post* and *The Wall Street Journal* have achieved reputations as competent choniclers of daily events.

Card Catalogues, of course, list the books (and in some places, bound periodicals, pamphlets, etc.) available in any single library. Usually, books are catalogued alphabetically according to author, title and subject and by virtue of a numbering system are located for the reader. Thus, if he wished a book by Egbert Erudite entitled *The Many Moods of Mount Rainier,* the researcher could look under *Erudite* or *Many Moods of Mount Rainier* or *Mountains.* In each place, he would find a card carrying essentially the same information, including a number in the upper left-hand corner telling him where the book is stored.

Knowing where to look for information is only the first part of the communicator's task, however. How he uses the source and what value he places on what he uses is the real test of an educated man. It is important, for example, to use an Encyclopedia only to obtain a broad view of the subject, gather insights into its relation to other subjects and secure additional source citations. Periodical and newspaper information should be used to gather more details and interpretations while specialized books and essays should be used to provide deeper and more reflective treatments. And the information gathered regardless of the sources employed, should be recorded accurately on note cards.

All serious professionals, whether in business or education, rely heavily on the card system to record important information. Cards unlike notebook paper can be conveniently shuffled and reshuffled to suit changing patterns; cards can be used for single ideas or categories while notebook paper is not so conveniently employed. If each card were titled with temporary subcategories, preliminary information can be gathered and stored with less random activity. Moreover, if each card were coded by letter or number to match a system detailed on a master card, one would be spared the labor of recording the entire source name on each card. Thus, one card would be set aside as a major bibliographical card on which the full title, author, place and date of publication were recorded. Opposite each source listed, the research could be a number or a letter. Thereafter, each card carrying information drawn from any of the sources shown on the master card would bear the number or letter assigned that source. With this system, the researcher is required to note only the specific page number in addition to the idea itself. Finally, all information should be recorded verbatim and set off by quotation marks to remind the researcher that paraphrases, if used, should be constructed only in the stage before organization of the outline.

Good Will

Supported by integrity and strengthened by competence, the ability to communicate effectively is made applicable by the important quality of good will. It affects the communicative act in two ways: influencing the disposition of the listener and modifying the speaker's management of tools. From the time of the first philosophical truth, it has been recorded that humans appear predisposed to return kindness with kindness, compassion with compassion, charity with charity. The speaker who, through the selection and treatment of his topic and the nature of his style and the management of the occasion, inspires his listener's good will has already progressed more than halfway toward his goal. This is the quality which neutralizes malice, compromises hate, removes indifference and motivates acceptance.

A speaker armed with insult and outrage and reflecting an insolent, overbearing, supercilious, reproachful or indifferent attitude will be rejected outright. On the other hand, a speaker who demonstrates a knowledge of his audience and, because of it, a concern for their welfare and a respect for their capabilities will tend to be accepted by that audience.

Supported by integrity, strengthened by competence and made applicable by good will, the ability to communicate becomes a power no other can give.

AUDIENCE ANALYSIS

The ultimate purpose of all communication is *audience response*. The very term audience is drawn from the presence of auditors; it refers particularly to a congregation of humans who came to hear the spoken word.

Despite a tradition of concern for uncovering the mysteries that control the behavior of the earwitnesses around him, the average person preparing to make a presentation will think more about himself than about his listeners. The problems that occupy most of his time will be those associated with his nervousness, the importance of the task, selection and preparation of audio-visual aids and the like.

Yet, with proper reflection, even the most elementary speaker will realize that the solution to each of these problems varies with each audience. Sportsmen diagnose and act according to the strengths and weaknesses of a specific opponent while attempting to apply the principles of their sport; medical doctors prescribe for specific patients though they apply general principles of medicine; psychiatrists spend much, if not most, of their time analyzing the peculiar difficulties of the individual client before drawing from their training and experience to determine how certain therapy will be applied. So, as noted in Figure 3, when man seeks to communicate he must always do so according to the peculiar attitudes, desires, goals and abilities of his specific "circle of witnesses" if he is to achieve his purpose.

Good audience analysis is the product of careful, systematic thought applied *before* and *during* the presentation. Easily the more extensive of the two, the analysis carried on before the presentation reflects much collecting and ordering of data from various sources for the purpose of selecting, arranging and developing the presentation. On the other hand, the analysis carried on during the presentation reflects dynamic thought applied to data drawn from immediate audience response for the purpose of modifying or rearranging the presentation. In each instance, the analysis must make use of proper sources and specific kinds of information.

Audience Analysis Before the Presentation

Prior to the presentation, as much information as possible should be obtained to enable the speaker to prepare efficiently. Such information is best secured from sources beyond those noted in the earlier portion of this chapter. These include information from previous speakers, from associates of the proposed auditors, from meetings, from official records, and from popular as well as specialized publications which may carry details and general observations about individual auditors or the group to which they belong.

Perhaps the most awkward source of relevant information about the listener is the *questionnaire,* with the listener consciously supplying biographical material, about himself. To be effective, questionnaires ought to be brief, simple and discreet. If possible, personal contact explaining the nature of request should precede the administration of the questionnaire. And, finally, a greater percentage of return can be assured by providing the audience with a common time and place for the completion of the questionnaire. The average person finds it easier and less embarrassing to make out a questionnaire about his personal history if he is but one of forty people doing the same thing at the same time.

To this point, the discussion has been concerned with suggested sources of audience information which the speaker should avail himself of before preparing the presentation. Now, attention should be given to the *kinds* of information which should be obtained.

As mentioned earlier, regardless of the kind of information secured, a special attempt should be made to segregate fact from opinion. Too often otherwise-discerning speakers have expended needless time, money and effort preparing a presentation based on ill-founded opinions of the audience. This is not to say that opinion is of no value; carefully gathered and clearly labeled opinion can, over a period of time, achieve a consensus which is as important as fact. This is to say that, unless clearly marked, isolated opinion may be mistakenly used as fact to guide the preparation of a program.

Speakers can do a more efficient job of organizing programs and presentations if they know the *purpose* for which the audience is gathered. This purpose, whenever possible, should be phrased by the audience or an agency responsible for it. Again, needless error can be avoided by working with fact rather than assumptions. Occasionally, the speaker assumes that an audience is gathered for a particular purpose and organizes his material accordingly, only to find — and to his dismay — that he is in error and the presentation has failed because of it.

Knowledge concerning the *size* of the audience will often determine certain aspects of selection, organization, development and delivery of the message. When speaking to a small, intimate group the speaker might profitably include more details than when speaking to large, unstable audiences. Applying this thought to matters of development, one can easily note that certain audio-visual aids are best suited to large audiences while others should never be used with audiences over fifteen or twenty.

If adaptation of the material to the audience is to be successful, it is imperative that the speaker know the needs, interests and experiences of his listeners. In the absence of specific information about these factors, the speaker can do a good job of deducing this knowledge from the *age range* of the audience. Intelligent men have been doing just that for well over two thousand years. Aristotle, writing almost three hundred and fifty years before Christ, recorded the major characteristics of men in their youth, in the prime of their life and in old age. He admonished the careful speaker to remember the differences in interest and experiences and plan his message accordingly.[3] Modern speakers would do well to heed the same admonition.

Though seemingly a minor matter, the careful speaker nevertheless considers the possible barriers to success created by the poor *physical condition* of his audients. It can be assumed, of course, that most persons are normal. However, such an assumption should not lead one to the point of excluding every other possibility. Very frequently in order to insure the success of the presentation, special seating arrangements have to be made to preserve the dignity of listeners who have special problems of hearing or seeing. A well-organized, well-prepared presentation is worthless unless it can be seen and heard by those for whom it has been intended.

As with physical matters, it can be assumed that the majority of audiences are composed of persons who enjoy a normal *psychological* state. Nevertheless, every normal individual has his special hopes, desires and prejudices and unless the speaker is conversant with those held by his listeners, he may unwittingly offend and antagonize; equally

---

[3]Lane Cooper, *The Rhetoric of Aristotle* (New York: D. Appleton-Century Co., 1932), pp. xx-xxi.

significant, he will lose the advantage of locating the "doors to the audience's mind." Among other things, the speaker should strive to determine the listener's attitudes (pro or con) towards the company or organization represented by him; the program, project or idea he discusses; his personality and the audio-visual aids he uses.

The listener's concept of *status* or his perception of his role in any given situation is also important knowledge for the speaker to gather. Properly defined, it will enable the speaker to select appropriate examples, language, tone and general demeanor.

In addition, the careful speaker considers the *previous activities* of his potential listener. Will his previous activities render the audient restless, bored, hostile, or indifferent? Has he been listening to four or five presentations prior to yours? Will he listen to three more after yours? Has he just eaten? Obviously, the answers to these and similar questions may very well direct the course of preparation for the talk.

Finally, the speaker should attempt to discover the listener's prejudices toward general matters of living such as politics, religion and recreational interests.

Also of importance is the knowledge of the listener's *capabilities*. More than years in school, this category should reveal the nature and scope of an individual's thought patterns. Is he habitually mesmerized by detail? Would he be at home with generalization and abstraction? Is much background or preparatory material needed to facilitate understanding and/or acceptance? Has the listener's past prepared him as an effective participant in situations of the sort being planned? Naturally, knowing something of the listener's training and experience will help the speaker secure answers to such important questions and thus avoid needless barriers in his quest for successful communication.

So much, then, for a discussion of the sources and kinds of information about the audience which speakers should seek before the presentation. The remaining part of this chapter will be devoted to the sources and kinds of information about the audience which the speaker should seek during the presentation.

Audience Analysis During the Presentation

A very important part of every efficient, dynamic operation — whether by machine or by man — is the control exercised by a feedback system. By carrying on a continuous evaluation of what *is* being done as compared with what *ought* to be done, the efficient organism or machine directs itself toward its ultimate task with a minimal amount of wasted effort. Unless he reacted to the hundreds of sensory stimuli sent into his brain to help direct his course of action, the average man would be of little value to himself or to the society to which he belonged as a civilized or social being. And yet, such persons do exist — some of them take the form of parents, teachers, researchers and salesmen. The one characteristic they share is that they "put out according to plan regardless of immediate conditions." The effective parent, teacher, researcher and salesman "puts out according to plan *unless* immediate conditions dictate otherwise." In a word, the effective communicator recognizes, appreciates, and uses feedback, which is the main tool of audience analysis *during* the presentation.

The most important source of information regarding audience reaction to a presentation is, of course, the audience itself. Whatever the mode of audience reaction, the speaker should be aware of the fact that his *eyes* and *ears* furnish him with most of the information to be gathered in such situations.

Doubtless the eyes play an important role in helping the speaker estimate the degree of his success or failure. By watching his audience carefully, the speaker can determine what portion of his message should be expanded or deleted, what aspect of his delivery needs to be modified, what listeners are or will be obstacles and so forth. Conversely, the nature and scope of a speaker's eye contact very often serve to inform the audience about his degree of sincerity, competence and good will. Most listeners feel uneasy in the presence of a speaker who continually averts his eyes; others are inclined to reject him and his proposal. The efficient speaker realizes that information gained through visual contact is as essential to a good presentation as the examples he uses to demonstrate his points.

This is also true of hearing. The speaker must be acutely aware of sounds emanating from the audience which are other than speech sounds. Restlessness, side conversations, excessive coughing and applause are clues which the good communicator uses to guide his adjustment of material and delivery. Moreover, the sense of hearing furnishes the speaker with an obvious opportunity to monitor what he is saying. Too often presentations are rendered impotent by virtue of an unedited remark offered by a speaker who was not listening to himself.

In addition to the main sources of information already cited which enable the speaker to analyze the audience during his presentation, there are subliminal cues or impressions from sensory stimuli. These are things one feels about audience attitude without knowing why.

Of the kinds of information mentioned previously under the section dealing with audience analysis before the presentation, size and age-range estimates could most obviously be altered as a result of an on-the-spot analysis. Less obvious is the fact that other categories can be modified in this way.

Keen observation by a sensitive speaker can also confirm or deny previous estimates of the physical state of the listener. Most eye glasses and hearing aids can be seen equally well by trained or untrained speakers, but only the trained, sensitive speaker can detect the habitual, prolonged squint or the unnatural tilt of the head as symptoms of impaired vision and audition. It is also true that the competent communicator will recognize and use cues in the form of exaggerated posture, facial expressions and incongruous behavior patterns (excessive doodling, whispering, dozing) to adapt his presentation to the immediate condition of his listener.

Less susceptible to on-the-spot analysis is audience prejudice regarding politics, religion and hobbies. For information about such interests, the speaker must rely mainly upon the analysis made "by the smell of the lamp" prior to the presentation. As regards audience attitude toward such things as the occasion, the program, the concept or the speaker, some aid is affected through on-the-spot analysis. In fact, it is conceivable that the immediate analysis would be of much more value than the prior analysis for determining such things as audience attitude toward the company, the speaker, the project, visual aids and the like. At times, also, the speaker may note that the audience wishes to remain on a formal or informal basis. The speaker may aid his cause by adjusting to the mood established by the audience. One method of doing so is to use the name or title of various listeners in the presentation (with discretion) and/or during any question-and-answer period.

The speaker must continually evaluate cues to find answers to such questions as: Is he listening? Is he bored? Has he understood? Is he convinced? The only valid answers for such questions are drawn largely from the immediate response of the listener.

SUMMARY

The skilled speaker recognizes the need for analyzing his own strengths and weaknesses regarding his ability as a persuader. Toward this end, he strives to define and maintain his integrity as related to each communicative experience. Moreover, he analyzes and maintains a high level of competence on each occasion by making wise use of relevant experience, training and research which strengthen his good will.

Since the ultimate purpose of all communication is audience response, competent speakers should make every effort to engage in an analysis of their audiences. This necessary analysis is actually twofold: (1) that engaged in prior to the presentation; (2) that engaged in during the presentation. Both require a knowledge of definite sources and kinds of information desired. Sources for prior analysis include permanent audience files, previous speakers, associates of listeners, formal meetings, personnel records, official publications, general publications and questionnaires. Sources for analyses conducted during the presentation include eyes, ears and subliminal cues. Kinds of information sought include audience purpose, size, names, age range, physical condition, psychological condition and capabilities.

PRACTICAL REMINDERS

Propositions

Speaker

1. A good speaker maintains a continuous evaluation of his source materials in the areas of training, experience and research.

2. A good speaker maintains a healthy skepticism of all conclusions drawn by himself and his sources.

3. A good speaker maintains an "illusion of the first time" whenever he seeks to engage in serious communication with his family and friends.

4. Speakers who generate a feeling of respect and sincere concern for the audience are generally more successful than those who manifest indifference.

Audience

1. The single most important phase of presentation is audience analysis.

2. Although susceptible to valid generalizations about people, each audience has its own special psychology and *must be analyzed separately.*

3. Intelligent, critical audients are more readily persuaded by presentations which expose various sides of a problem as well as recommended solution.

4. Intelligent, critical audients must be given opportunity and time to draw occasional inferences.

5. With small audiences particularly, explicit adaptation by each speaker (to individual listeners, preceding speakers, immediate psycho-

physical conditions) tends to promote more rapid and lasting favorable impressions.

6. Listeners already favorably disposed toward the speaker, message or program should be spread through the audience rather than seated in a group.

7. Attention and interest of listeners manifest themselves in waves rather than at some particular time during the presentation; *they must, therefore, be considered throughout the presentation.*

8. Women recall and retain less of a given message than men.

9. Women do not evaluate messages as critically as men do.

10. More intelligent audiences are less influenced by speaker prestige than other audiences.

Exercises

1. What attitude is revealed by the speaker in the following instances:

    a. "The bottle is half full." vs. "The bottle is half empty."

    b. "I have paid $20,000 on a $40,000 home." vs. "I owe $20,000 on a $40,000 home."

    c. "Why were those left out?" vs. "Why were those included?"

    d. "Speech is self-expression." vs. "Speech is social interaction."

    e. "I have an hour to rest." vs. "I must get up in one hour."

2. Speaker Research (see page 46)

3. After a talk has been prepared and outlined to be delivered to one audience, note what specific changes in language, examples or order would have to be made if the same subject were presented to a group of middle-aged women, an audience composed of career men in the Armed Forces or a group of high school seniors.

4. Revise Lincoln's Gettysburg Address so that it can be delivered to a community of Negroes and whites in a large American metropolis.

5. What possible effective adjustments might a good speaker make when, in the middle of his talk, approximately one fourth of the audience leaves? When fifty or sixty persons are ushered into the room and proceed to fill up various empty seats throughout the room?

Readings

Andersen, Martin P., Lewis, Wesley and Murray, James, *The Speaker and His Audience*, New York: Harper & Row, Publishers, 1964.

Hollingsworth, H. L., *The Psychology of the Audience*, New York: American Book Company, 1935.

Hovland, Carl J., Janis, Irving L. and Field, Peter B., *Communication and Persuasion*, New Haven, Conn.: Yale University Press, 1953.

2. Speaker Research

Name:
Section:
Date:

Topic	Answers			Conclusion
	Source #1	Source #2	Source #3	
1. How many persons in the world speak the following languages? Italian Swedish Swahili Russian				
2. How many British soldiers were involved in the battle of Lexington and Concord? How many Americans?				
3. How many troops did the United States have in Vietnam from January to December, 1965? How many North Vietnamese troops were involved in that period?				

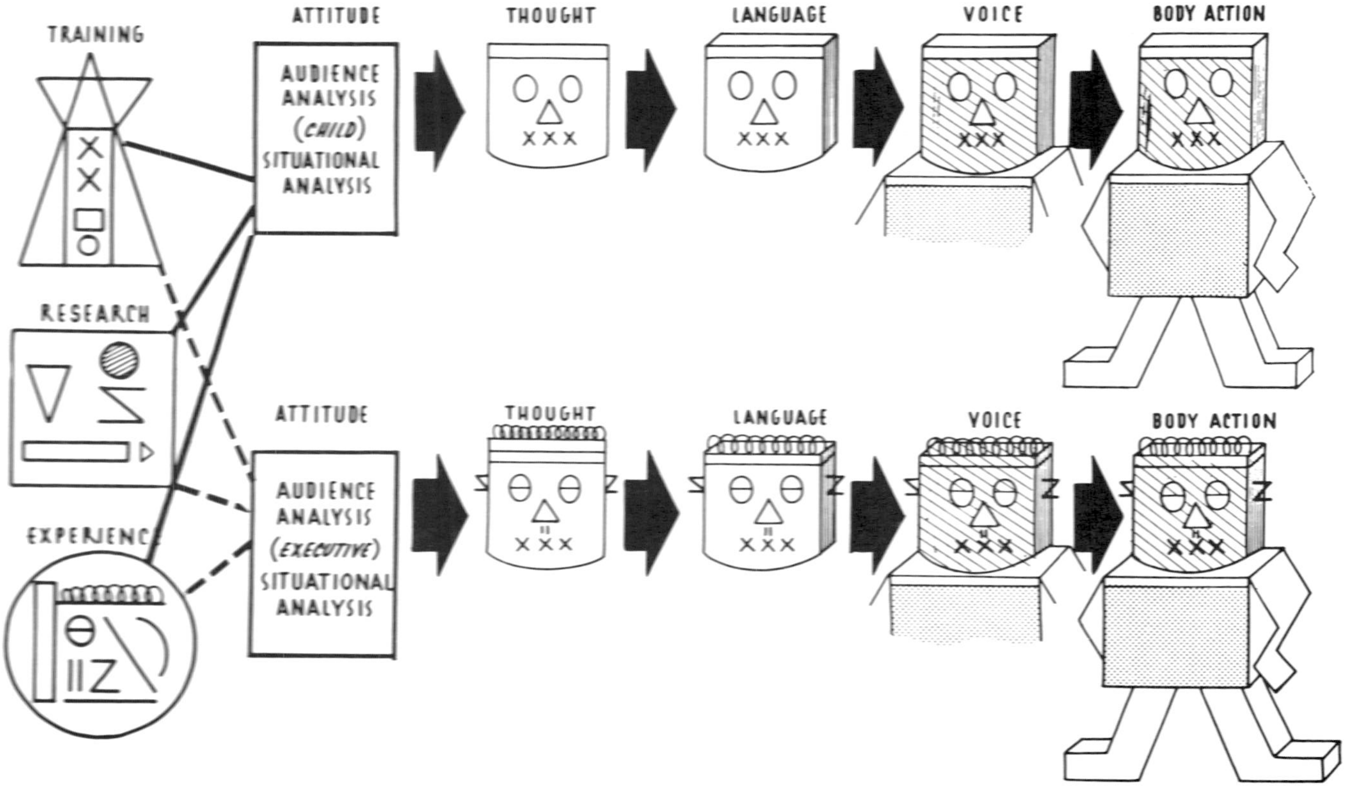

TRAINING
RESEARCH
EXPERIENCE
ATTITUDE
AUDIENCE ANALYSIS (CHILD) SITUATIONAL ANALYSIS
THOUGHT
LANGUAGE
VOICE
BODY ACTION
ATTITUDE
AUDIENCE ANALYSIS (EXECUTIVE) SITUATIONAL ANALYSIS
THOUGHT
LANGUAGE
VOICE
BODY ACTION

FIGURE 3

Hovland, Carl J., *Personality and Persuasibility*, New Haven, Conn.: Yale University Press, 1959.

Krech, David, Crutchfield, Richard S. and Ballachey, Egerton L., *Individual in Society*, New York: McGraw-Hill Book Company, 1962.

Martin, Harold C., *The Logic and Rhetoric of Exposition*, New York: Henry Holt & Company, Inc., 1958.

Chapter 4

SKILLS OF THE SPEAKER:
Message Analysis

Having considered the analysis of speaker-listener roles in the communicative experience, attention is now directed toward the third important ingredient: the message itself.

Principle A notes that effective speech is organized, meaningful and selectively particular. As a corollary to this, it might be said that effective speech is purposeful speech. Throughout the years, scholars from Plato to John Quincy Adams have attempted to classify the various speech purposes and have generally agreed upon three: entertainment, information and persuasion. As has already been observed, this text assumes it is more advantageous to treat all oral communication as having persuasion as its goal. The more subtle nuances which identify certain speaking experiences as entertaining but not informative and others as informative but not persuasive should be left for more advanced study. With this in mind, the following discussion emphasizes clarity, development and style as significant factors in the probative force of any oral message.

CLARITY

Every act of communication can be placed upon a continuum of clarity from the one extreme represented by a column of numbers with a stated sum to that of a child defining love. Oral communication has at times the dual function of clarifying the speaker's ideas for both speaker and listener. Many times true understanding is acquired by the speaker only after his attempt to communicate with others. Primarily, however, the speaker's task is to make clear the ideas, moods and attitudes he wishes to convey to the listener. The substance of the speaker's conversation should mean to the listener what it means to the speaker. In this period of great confusion, of thousands of distractions all calling for the average person's attention, of much sound and less sense, a speaker who wishes attention must express himself clearly enough to be understood at once. Few listeners have the time, inclination or ability to sort through a jumble of words or unravel hopelessly tangled thoughts. Clarity in the meaning of a speaker's message may be affected by the nature of the subject and by its order of presentation.

Theme

An effective speaker must have some specific point to which all his comments are directed. Every act is thus founded on a central idea, feeling, mood and so forth. It is the intellectual equivalent of deciding which target to shoot for in directing one's efforts during a hunt. Physically, economically and psychologically it would be a waste to attempt to focus on two targets at the same time. While it may appear obvious and trivial, in everyday communication nothing is more common than to see this point ignored or forgotten. Conversations drip with four or five different topics jumbled together like so many pieces of laundry in an automatic washer. Their only relationship is that they are contained within the same receptacle in the same period of time — and perhaps they are soiled to the same degree.

Our laws demonstrate the need for curtailing this confusion by requiring courts and legislative bodies to specify in separate fashion each issue to be discussed. Parliamentary procedure allows for this clear definition of issues and provides the means whereby a clear sequence of topics and related discussions may be allowed. Yet, in most daily discussion, nothing provides for this needed precision except the sensitive habits of either speaker or listener. For example, a speaker may be endeavoring to discuss, formally or informally, the merits of land condemnation of offshore drilling procedures, but the listener has shifted to condemnation of private industrial corporations. It would be an unwise use of time and energy to continue the discussion unless the speaker firmly restricts the discussion to one theme or the other. Again, a speaker may be telling a chamber of commerce group that Standard Oil of California is dedicated to the goals of service, research and economy but the greatest of these is service. The major portion of the discussion must focus on the assertion that service is the most important goal; the speaker should not get sidetracked into developing the important qualities of research and economy. These should be discussed only as their relative merits demonstrate the greater importance of service.

Incidental themes, arising naturally out of the discussion, often become so entangled with the main thought that they cloud it. And yet, just as often, these issues are not essential to the main idea. Definition is probably the best example of a minor issue which could easily mislead the speaker and confuse the listener. In attending to the merits of private enterprise versus public ownership, many speakers become bogged down in the definition of terms. The goal is to persuade the listener on the merits of private enterprise not to school him on the intricacies of subtle legal definitions. It is enough to let him know what most people mean by the term and to let him know that the term will be used in this way. Most of the time and energy should then be directed toward supporting the declared issue.

Many speakers have failed to achieve their desired end simply because of the listener's inability to determine the exact nature of the topic being discussed.

Order

Structure, in the human society, is part and parcel of most experience available to the normal individual. From the architecture of cities to the architecture of feelings and thoughts, the average person is predisposed toward the acceptance of form and the rejection of the formless. As noted earlier, man as an organizing animal reacts to material presented in disorganized fashion by rejecting it or organizing it according to his own prejudices. While the degree of form or structure varies with each phenomenon, no phenomenon of life whether animate or inanimate appears to the individual as completely devoid of order. Each reflects a time, space or logical order. Such form or structure or order is, of course, an inherent and important part of the phenomenon of communication, from the most basic sequence of introduction, body and conclusion to the more sophisticated concerns of the sequence of ideas within these basic parts.

One who spends his life haphazardly gathering impressions, opinions and facts and who communicates them in the same way they were gathered is like a builder who spends years gathering all sorts of exotic and special materials for construction of a mighty building but never attempts to arrange them in an order which will insure strength, beauty or convenience. It is not enough to select and gather materials for communication. They must be ordered and used as the occasion demands.

In oral communication, even more than in written communication, order plays an important role in deciding the degree of success or failure. In the instances where individual words fail to convey a clear meaning to the listener, for example, a knowledge of the larger order or design of the speaker helps. Such knowledge comes, first of all, from the order of the sentence in which the word is placed. Meaning is revealed by each word's association with other words which perform certain functions in the sentence. Thus, "red" by itself means several things; in the sentence "John is a red," its meaning is more precisely prescribed. Further, the meaning of individual words is indicated by the position and function played by the sentence in the larger unit, the paragraph. In this way, we are able to deduce the meanings of words used inaccurately or ambiguously by children, foreigners, the uneducated and even the careless speaker.

The order or design of a speaker's message is revealed most obviously by his own description of it before and during his act of communication. Thus, if a speaker says he will discuss the impact of the aerospace industry on the nation, the community and the individual citizen, the listener "sets" himself to receive information in each of these areas and in this sequence. Less obviously, the speaker's design is revealed by the sequence of his discussion, the time and place in which it is given and by a knowledge of the events leading up to the communication. As parents, by way of example, we note from the initial comments of flattery and from the unusual concern for our welfare that our children will soon request favors. As executives, we assume that a meeting arranged by a representative of labor just prior to the expiration of a contract will be concerned — even indirectly — with the present and future conditions of the contract.

In most instances of oral communication, two major types of order function most effectively and these are best revealed in the development of the selected themes. These basic forms of reason include *deduction* which is a movement from general concepts (of time, order or other associations) to specific instances, and *induction* which involves a logical movement from specific instances to general categories related to those instances.

DEVELOPMENT

Having clearly defined and limited his topic, then having selected the relevant subpoints, the speaker must now move to select a method of demonstrating the connection between various subpoints and between the subpoints and the main points which make up his theme. Without abandoning the main idea, he must summon other ideas which will confirm, strengthen and clarify it. Held together by the main ideas, the supporting illustrations and examples form a meaningful pattern. Without such a clear relationship, without a logical association, the main ideas and supporting examples used by a speaker represent little more than a meaningless jumble much like the beads of a broken necklace. Simply stated, an effective communicator is able to give reasons for his statements and his actions.

The logical association referred to as *deduction* is most generally identified or demonstrated through the use of a syllogism, or an argument which has three closely interrelated parts. Thus, one might argue:

> All Italians are hot-tempered
> Mario is an Italian
> Therefore, Mario is hot-tempered.

However, no one speaks *habitually* in syllogistic fashion and very few *ever* speak in this way.[1] As an artificial device (invented by Aristotle) constructed to test some of the more formal types of oral communication, it achieved great popularity. Unfortunately, its identity as a test was lost in the surge of popularity and it soon became a part of the material taught to students of speech as an ideal form of communication. This is obviously a serious mistake since, once away from the classroom, the student soon learns of its impractical qualities and drops it from further consideration of any kind. *It should be learned, but only as a test to be applied to the real form of deduction used in oral communication: the enthymeme.*[2]

The enthymeme is a kind of syllogism. It is frequently used in communication and generally takes the form of a conclusion welded to a statement from which the conclusion came. Thus, "If he has never played baseball, he is not an American." The conclusion ("he is not an American") is offered because of the earlier observation ("if he has never played baseball") plus an unstated belief ("All Americans play baseball"). Other examples demonstrate the same *assumed connection*:

Blessed are the meek, for they shall inherit the earth.	Conclusion: Blessed are the meek. Because: They (the meek) shall inherit the earth. Unstated: All who inherit the earth are blessed.
Someone must have died because the flag is at half-mast.	Conclusion: Someone must have died. Because: The flag is at half-mast. Unstated: Whenever someone dies the flag is put at half-mast.

---

[1] John Locke, *An Essay Concerning Human Understanding*, Book IV, selected by Mary W. Calkins (LaSalle, Ill.: The Open Court Publishing Company, 1949), pp. 267.

[2] Most generally pronounced *en-the-meem*.

The possibility of error, of drawing false conclusions, becomes more obvious when the enthymeme *is restated to include the unstated assumptions.* When exceptions are drawn up for the statements and when the connections between statements are tested to determine whether it shows what it purports to show, the concept is properly tested.

The oral communicator who is serious about improving his ability to communicate effectively would do well to apply the basic test suggested by the previous discussion; he would do very well to apply it *when he assembles his materials as a speaker* and when he, as a listener, *receives the materials assembled by another speaker.*

Closely allied to the matter of deduction (usually observed as enthymemes in oral conversation) is the *inductive* mode of logical association. This, as noted earlier, is the process of piling one instance upon another until an obvious conclusion is forthcoming. Its most perfect form is complete enumeration — a one hundred per cent listing of instances, a perfect survey omitting not one single example. As with the syllogism of the deductive form of reasoning, the perfect enumeration is rarely if ever a part of inductive reasoning as applied to oral communication. Rather, induction is most commonly identified as the example or the analogy.

Thus, one hears reasoning when he hears, "I think the Bramas will win the league championship since they have won it every year for the last ten years." So, too, in the situation where he hears, "Those students at Tukwila University are not to be trusted since those two cheating scandals came out." Testing this form of reasoning amounts to finding exceptions in the same materials used by the speaker (other years when the Bramas did *not* win; known students from Tukwila University who did *not* cheat) or by noting that the examples used for the conclusion were not typical.

The analogy is thought to be literal if it is based upon some actual example, or figurative if based upon some hypothetical relationship defined by the speaker. Either way, it is an indirect way of concluding something from prior experience; it assumes similar results will follow similar causes in situations which are quite similar. Thus, if one got hives twice after eating crabmeat, he would probably avoid crabmeat. When he moves to avoid shrimp as well, he gives evidence of reasoning by analogy. He moved from defining a series of likenesses between two things and an unpleasant experience associated with one of them, *to the conclusion* that the second thing will also produce unpleasantness. Notice that, while this movement of thought shows many possibilities for error, it is not as gross as a movement which would go from crabmeat to all edible things.

The main weakness with this type of reasoning is that as the similarities became fewer and more indirect, the argument gets proportionally weaker. Argument by analogy always assumes there are more similarities than dissimilarities or that similarities are more important than dissimilarities. Very often, a few similar but unimportant theses are offered as evidence for a conclusion, when the actual value of a conclusion depends on theses not stated.

The inductive mode, then, attempts to abstract from similar details in each instance and infer a generalization.

It should be evident, even at this point in the discussion, that the speaker's message carries probative force or persuasive power by its clarity and logical development. It should be clear, also, that the core of human reasoning is made up of fact and inferences drawn from other facts. These inferences may be drawn by induction or deduction but, however they are arrived at, it is important that the connecting threads be strong, direct and intact. In proportion as they are, and are demonstrated, the listener will more readily understand and accept the conclusion.

Oddly enough, we pretend to demand logic in others, but rarely do we examine the soundness of our own conclusions. For this reason, arguments which are most purely logical, that is, quite obvious in their logical relationships, often tend to be put aside since the contrast between what the listener hears and what he knows he offers, casts an unfavorable light upon himself. The myth that "man is a logical animal" was started by man. More a hope than a fact, this myth has served to confound as much as to help. More truthfully, man is an animal capable of both rational and nonrational activity. Relation of logical and psychological materials is always tenuous. That the coexistence of both categories exists in the most intelligent persons has long been established. Superstitious scientists, fanatically religious college professors, prejudiced judges and the like, substantiate the existence of this phenomenon. Society schools its young in the hope that the logical will dominate the illogical — most of the time. Should the reverse occur, the individual is segregated formally by commitment to an institution or informally by ostracism from the various circles of society.

Reason alone has rarely influenced anyone. "The facts," if they could be universally accepted, would always need some motivating agent to make them palatable to a certain audience at a certain time. If reason alone were sufficient, then we would need no schools, churches, industries and so forth; a mere citation of the facts would lead to the only possible conclusion. But even with the same set of facts, men arrive at different conclusions. The smoker and nonsmoker, the drinker and nondrinker, the Catholic and Protestant, the Chevron customer and the Shell customer do not disagree on matters of fact. They disagree, rather, on the conclusions drawn from those facts, or on matters not even a part of any related experience.

It has long been true of human activity that the "logical proposes and the psychological disposes." No sooner does the listener catch the speaker's *psychological* emphases — to share his likes, dislikes, indignations and joys — than he assumes the speaker's point of view. Psychological motivations — appeals to hopes, fears, desires, prejudices — have rarely caused a lasting persuasion when operating alone. "Nothing," we are reminded by the European adage, "is so rapid as the drying of a teardrop; nothing so transient as states of bliss." Nevertheless, such appeals used wisely have caused great refinement in the actions of men. Few people have ever been persuaded to pursue a certain course of action or to abandon another without having that action related to gratification of some need. Whether it is done because it is honorable or good or profitable or necessary, it is done because it fulfills that particular need experienced by the listener. One such need, little appreciated by many scholars of democratic societies, is the need to rely on *authority*.[3]

As has been pointed out, dependence upon authority increases as the society becomes more complex; the more removed the average person is from original experiences, the more he depends upon the experience of others. No man can live long enough to acquire by direct experience all of the needed information to operate efficiently in today's world; more importantly, few live long enough to understand such information. To develop as rational social beings, men become indebted to others for everything about the past and for most things concerning the present. Few of us have directly experienced certain aspects of farming, warfare, space flight, travel to Russia, medical advancement and the like. None of us personally knew Jesus, Columbus or George Washington, yet because of the testimony of others, we operate as though we did. Anyone we feel indebted to is treated as an authority. If enough persons are indebted to the same person, he becomes an expert.

The importance of authority in everyday activity is significant even in the most democratic societies. The relationship of child to parent, student to teacher, worker to boss and citizen to administrator demonstrates the role and influence of authority in our lives. There is an evident role played by testimonials in selling everything from religion to

---

[3]H. Gilkinson, S. Paulson, D. Sikkink, "Effects of Order and Authority in An Argumentative Speech," *Quarterly Journal of Speech* (April, 1954), pp. 183-192.

cigarettes. Generally speaking, it is more difficult for the average listener to reject a proposition, plan or program when it comes to him clearly, when it is in language which is meaningful and when it bears the stamp of approval from someone highly respected and admired. Ideas rarely have force standing alone. They are believed or disbelieved only when they are advanced by an individual or an institution. The power value of ideas, therefore, is partially determined by the authorities supporting them.

Another significant but not generally recognized need, is that which causes most listeners to seek out and believe those things for which they already carry *conviction*. And, accordingly, they seem to expect the same from others, particularly of a speaker who wishes to claim a portion of their time, money or effort. Ministers who reveal that they would rather be playing golf than delivering "the same old message," doctors who while inhaling a cigarette try to convince patients that smoking is bad for the health, teachers who discourse on the value of personal conferences with students while never arranging them for their own students, all demonstrate a certain lack of conviction which the sensitive auditor finds difficult to ignore. Few persons would be willing to accept the adage "Do as I say not as I do," particularly when it accompanies urgent pleas on important matters.

A speaker wishing to be effective will recognize the importance of his own convictions in any of his attempts to move others toward understanding or action. Equivocation, excessive modification and the like generally serve to confuse and confound the listener. Few things are more objectionable to an audience than a good idea associated with a mediocre speaker. On the other hand, a seemingly mediocre idea assumes other proportions when offered by a speaker convinced of its worth and ready to describe this worth to the listener. False enthusiasm will rarely survive as a moving force with extended exposure before sensitive listeners. People are not inclined to share their time with others who seem to believe one thing but who speak on another. On occasion, the wise speaker makes a decision not to talk with a certain group at a certain time on a certain subject because of his own lack of conviction and closeness to the ideas, programs or policies.

In addition to such psychological aids as authority and conviction, the speaker can add to the value of his message by efficacious *humor*. Aside from visual aids, the most misused of the speaker's forces is humor. Properly employed, humor can make the difference between a communication which is lived and one which is endured.

It is now commonplace among experts that the essence of humor is incongruity; it is the revelation of the unexpected. In the clash of two incongruities, there appears what has been called "the flash of humor." These incongruities may be in matters of time, form and substance related to people, places, things, events *and the relationships among these*. But all individuals are not equal in their ability to detect the existence of incongruity or to appreciate the resultant "flash" emerging from a confrontation of two incongruities. For this reason, some people are thought of as being devoid of a sense of humor; others are labeled as highly sensitive to humor. For this reason, also, there are various levels of humor.

The most basic form of humor, appreciated by all but the most common among the primitive tribes and the uneducated in modern society, is that demonstrated by physical incongruity. The man who walks with a gait not common to most individuals, the fat woman who tries to sit on a small stool, the person sporting a pie on his face, all these situation can be recognized and appreciated as humor by the most uncultivated mind. The more sophisticated level of humor is that which involves less direct behavior and more symbolic concerns. As an individual or a society becomes more cultured, as either begins to substitute symbolic processes for the direct processes wherever possible, appreciation of verbal humor is made more real. The ironical or sarcastic, a pun, quip or story represent the refined development of the more sophisticated level of humor.

A sense of humor has often been looked on as an infallible sign of a healthy personality. Whether or not this is true, men believe their fellows reveal the extent of their mental and emotional flexibility through habitual patterns of humor. They appear to single out the individual who is capable of noting certain subtle relationships, has the willingness to remove himself from immersion in the immediate situation, and can appreciate the build-up of tension required for the recognition of the "flash" which designates true humor. The oral communicator exercising control over himself and certain aspects of his environment. helps to create for his listener a special and brief moment of truth. This he does by working artistically with the materials *in the immediate communicative situation* to arrange for the juxtaposition of two or more incongruities. Then, allowing the listener only bits and pieces of this arrangement through a gradual unfolding process, the speaker suddenly and precisely reveals the "flash" of complete vision and humor is experienced.

This ability has benefits for both the individual and his society. From the standpoint of the individual, it enables him to achieve the perspective necessary to a better understanding of any event, person institution or process.[4] When one sees the humorous aspect of these things, it is as though he has seen the dark side of the moon and thus a deeper appreciation of its true nature. The most obvious case in point is the person who can see humor in some of his own thoughts, attitudes and actions. Armed with this insight, he can maintain balance in his relationships and worth in his activities; equipped with a sense of discernment, he provides himself with the priceless medicine for physical pain and mental torment. And so with the society which fosters and values humor. Throughout history the remark has been made that without the ability to laugh at itself, a society is doomed to an early death. When jokes cease to be made, when laughter is no longer heard and when the list of subjects considered to be above humor continues to grow, concern for the life of society arises. Whether in individuals or societies, humor is most troublesome to the insecure and the ill.

But as with medicine, humor can be misapplied. It can be rendered useless (and sometimes harmful) because of the person using it, the patient to whom it is applied, or the time, place and circumstance of application. The respected oral communicator recognizes the difference between *planned* and *spontaneous* humor. Planned humor, whether in nonverbal form (dress, posture, gait, practical jokes, etc.) or in the verbal mode (stories and puns), has the advantage of control and places less strain on the speaker. On the other hand, planned humor is disadvantageous in most communicative situations because it is dated and carries an air of mechanization and remoteness which weakens its psychological value. Spontaneous humor, by contrast, has the greater psychological benefit because it is more fluid, dynamic, timely and personal. And yet, these are the very qualities which increase the speaker's chance of failure since all persons are not equally proficient in its use.

Generally speaking, speakers ought to avoid the canned story — particularly at the introduction. Contrary to popular opinion, there is no evidence to support the contention that it "gets the audience with you." As has been noted by the first principle discussed in Chapter 2, good communication is organized, meaningful and selectively particular. Most story jokes fulfill none of these qualities since, by their very nature, they relate to other times and other circumstances. Unless the speaker can make the relationship between the story and *all factors of the immediate situation* (listener, time, place, message, speaker) he should

---

[4]See John G. Fuller's column "Trade Winds," *The Saturday Review* (July 16, 1966), pp. 16-17. Also Evan Esar, *The Humor of Humor* (New York: Horizon Press, 1952), pp. 7-11.

avoid its use. Effective adaptation can be made, but as with other matters of consequence, it requires sensitivity, care and precision.

Adaptation of stories begins, of course, by changing names, places, dates and actions so that they come within the experience of the immediate listener. For example, in telling the well-known joke involving a sly dig the following possibilities exist:

Do you know that the brains of sell to researchers for as much as $10.00 a pound while those gotten from _____ cost as much as $25.00 a pound?

{ secretaries
doctors
lawyers
ministers
executives

Depending upon his audience, the speaker can inject the name of any group he wishes into the blank spot to secure maximum results. Thus, if speaking to educators, he might well inject *principal* or *dean* or *superintendent*. He would, accordingly, alter the first list to avoid mentioning the group reserved for the punch line which is, (in answer to the inevitable question why), "Do you know how many _____ it takes to get a pound of brains?" Similarly, one may alter the various phrases and sequence of phrases to suit his particular need. Note how one joke can be made to suit different listeners, occasions and so on.

I can't remember the name but the language   is familiar.
                                   breath
                                   pain
                                   aggressiveness
                                   boredom
                                   dogma

If one were speaking to an appreciative minister, rabbi, priest or nun, he could easily insert the word *faith* for a good "play" on the original version.

a group or profession
Do you know it takes 5 (*being joked about*) to replace a light bulb — one to hold the bulb and four to turn the ladder?

With all the possibilities for modification and adaptation of standard stories, the strongest type of humor remains the pun, quip, reversed proverb or story drawn from the immediate environment. The speech professor who, after hearing a long and embarrassing introduction about his achievements and prowess as a speaker, starts by saying, "Unaccustomed as I am to public speaking" does just that sort of thing.

So does the speaker who capitalizes upon accidents, noises and other distractions which occur during his presentation. But proficiency does not come simply by wishing; one must understand the importance of *timing* (adequate pausing and phrasing), *adaptation* and *practice* in this as in other aspects of the communicative process.

At an earlier point, the thought was expressed that people are influenced by their ability to understand and by their decisions to act because of the force brought upon them by the speaker, the message and the occasion. In terms of the message, it has been suggested that its force is carried by clarity, development and style. Having considered the pertinent parts of both clarity and development, the conscientious speaker moves to understand the intricacies of style or the proficient use of language.

STYLE

Effective use of language adds unquestioned force to the message and most of all to clarity. The words selected, the arrangement of these words and the artistic consideration of specialized functions of the various arrangements all contribute to make the message confused or clear, weak or forceful. The use of one type of language throughout an extended talk inevitably results in monotony and destroys the listener's interest and capacity to profit from the communication. Long and involved sentence structure unrelieved by colloquial language soon becomes tiresome; excessive slang also fatigues the mind and encourages it to wander. A linguistic style satiated with variety is deadly; a linguistic style so variable as to be inconsistent is bewildering. *One who sincerely wishes to communicate with another will construct a style which points as directly as possible to the idea or the feeling being expressed and nothing else.* He begins the construction by attending to his basic building material: words.

Words

As wonderful as speech is, it represents an attempt to make static that which is dynamic, to section off a part of a continuous panorama of experiences which are in the process of developing. As a fluid assumes the shape of its container, ideas and experiences take on the qualities of the pre-existing words used to describe them. By using words, one categorizes and in so doing removes or minimizes the unique features of the concepts or feelings. For this reason, the careful communicator works continually for a better appreciation of the words in his vocabulary and those available to him in the vocabulary of his society. The English speaking communities have well over one-half million words available to them, and as society progresses into new areas with new experiences, that number will increase. The average individual within these communities has a vocabulary of approximately ten thousand words and of these uses about two thousand in his habitual patterns of conversation. Difficulty arises because of the misuse of some words and the overuse of others.

The efficient speaker is aware that English provides him with some words which are *general* (designating classes of things or activities such as animal, fish, sports, etc.); some which are *specific* (designating units within the general classes such as dog, salmon, baseball, etc.); some which are *abstract* (designating qualities or states which exist nowhere but in the minds of the communicants such as righteous, republicanism, love, etc.); and others which are *concrete* (designating things and actions which can be and are regularly experienced such as boyhood, school, marriage, etc.). Even more helpful is the speaker's realization that whether general or specific, abstract or concrete words vary in their meanings according to the speaker, listener, time, place and the occasion associated with their use.

All words, in order to be included in the vocabulary of any society, must have (or have had) a *denotation*, that is, a meaning which many (or most) of the people in the society share with reasonable limits. In many societies, such meanings are noted in dictionaries which are compiled to record usage; they are not used to set standards. Thus, a stranger, or younger or relatively uneducated member in a society will put himself closer to his contemporaries by referring to the dictionary whenever he is unsure how a word is used. And so will the educated person profit, for meanings — even denotations — are in a constant state of flux. It can readily be seen that a speaker using the word *compact* must differentiate in its use much more carefully today than if he were speaking in 1945; an elderly person using *dashboard* to a teen-ager must be certain that the younger man shares his image of a place against which one places his foot when the horses start galloping with the carriage. In a few years, it is conceivable that some children may have to resort to the dictionary to find out what their grandparents mean when they speak of a *cow*. To make matters even more difficult, because many people have such imprecise denotations to begin with, only a very careful re-examination will bring them to their attention. Efficient communication is not possible without precise denotations of words. What, if any, is the difference in denotation between *aggravate* and *irritate*, *best* and *better*, *liberal* and *free*, *love* and *like*? Could these differences really alter understanding?

But even if the denotation of a word was sharp and clear to both speaker and listener, misunderstanding could still arise from the cloud of social and/or personal associations (*connotations*) trailing after it. If these associations are strong enough, the denotation is lost in a haze of specialized meanings which the speaker intends but the listener misses, or which the listener appends to what the speaker intends. Either way, the participants in the communicative situation are being driven apart while, on the surface, they appear to be intimate companions in thought. A somewhat detailed account of one such instance must answer for the thousands of others which occur daily. Suppose a speaker were addressing an audience of Christian religious workers on the subject of communication and, particularly, on the three aspects of life which are brought to bear by any speaker: experience, training and research. In approaching this point he could introduce it with the following:

> A speaker's efficiency is determined by his use of a trinity composed of experience, training and research.

Obviously, the use of the word *trinity* is perfectly in order since its denotation is tripart, triad or anything else representing an amalgamation of three discrete entities. But before this particular audience, the speaker would be ill advised to use such a word *because of the cloud* (or halo) *of religious associations which the listeners share* and which are completely apart from the legitimate meaning. On the other hand, if he were speaking to an audience composed of atheists, Moslems, or even a cross section of the world's population, his choice of *trinity* instead of a synonym would not be as hazardous. In less dramatic situations, the word *biweekly* could present as many confusions. Unless the speaker clearly differentiates between twice a week or once every two weeks, the listener might think one when the speaker intends the other.

In sum, the good speaker will make a definite word judgment in each instance of his oral communicative experiences. And such a judgment will always be made in terms of the propriety and effectiveness as *defined by the listener and the circumstances of the occasion* — not according to the speaker's experience.

Composition

The art of putting words together into meaningful patterns is referred to as composition. Here again, the good communicator is aware of the importance of order. Taken separately, words, like the pieces of a mosaic, are of minor interest only. After revealing their color and form, they cease to function. If, however, they are combined by a skilled person, they can produce a wonderful masterpiece. Handled by an unskilled person, they can only form a combination or grouping which is naive, confusing or with little meaning. The words cannot be pronounced in random fashion and still convey the speaker's ideas to the listener. In beginning societies, the accepted practice was to pronounce the most important parts of the idea first and follow these with the accessories. As ideas, subtle relationships of activity and refinements of feeling develop, more precise associations are demanded. The result is grammar. The natural order presents words in succession according to the desires of the speaker. The grammatical order presents words according to the relationship which they bear to each other. Thus, one order is specific and concerned only with the immediate idea being expressed and the other order is more general and is concerned with all ideas. It is important that every member of a speaking community knows enough of the basic rules of the game (and language is a game played according to rules previously agreed upon and not subject to immediate change) to avoid blunders which will encourage confusion and possible tragedy.

If the purpose of language is to convey thought or feeling, then whatever interferes with that purpose should be eliminated and whatever enhances it should be developed. In addition to having concern for basic rules of grammar, the effective speaker is aware of the length and complexity of his sentences. Since the listener cannot refer to what was said as easily as a reader can, and since the listener tends to be easily distracted when listening, the speaker must make certain his ideas are immediately intelligible. Proper words, well arranged, help to create this immediate intelligibility; short, uninvolved sentences help insure it. In oral practice, sentences from ten to twenty words long prove to be most effective. A common failing is to use sentences which are too long and to use a written rather than oral style. Too many words, too many clauses, too many parenthetical expressions and too many transitions are all communication barriers.

For purposes of variety, effective speakers endeavor to mix the two most basic forms of the sentence, the *periodic* and the *loose*. The periodic sentence presents the essentials of the idea at the end of its construction. The loose sentence, on the other hand, presents the essentials of the idea at the beginning of its construction and follows with the necessary modifiers. For example, note the samples:

Periodic	Loose
On a lonely road, in the middle of the night, one cold evening in December, *John was killed.*	*John was killed,* on a lonely road, in the middle of the night, one cold evening in December.
In an instance of this sort, without further thought, *Standard should sue.*	*Standard should sue,* in an instance of this sort, without further thought.

It can easily be seen that there are advantages to each form. The periodic arrangement is best for establishing a suspension of attention, for the marshalling of thoughts, for added emphasis. The loose structure is best for bringing matters to the fore more rapidly. It should be remembered that children, older persons and those more easily fatigued require shorter more direct sentences. But all audiences must have these sentences used in combination.

Linguistic Devices

For the most effective style, variety is indispensable. Periodic sentences mixed with loose sentences, comparisons mixed with contrasts, negations mixed with positive sentences, complex ideas interspersed with simple thoughts, all add to the individual speaker's force and effectiveness. Part of this variety, part of the ultimate sense of force is contributed to by figurative language. Wisely employed, figurative language is fresh, novel and serves to explain, illustrate and enforce ideas.

Unfortunately, figurative language is often considered too remote from natural speech to be of much use. Yet, this is precisely the language used in the course of everyday communication. Because people learn best by having an unknown thought, feeling or activity associated with one they already know about, figurative language (which provides a diagram for such associations) is readily accepted. This is especially true when one seeks to communicate about nonphysical matters, about matters of the mind. We begin, usually, by noting that the unknown object, idea or relationship is actually much like something we have already experienced. Thus, a comparison is born.

Figurative language is generally classified according to the type of association it stresses. There are examples which stress *resemblance*, those which emphasize *contiguity* of time or space and those which stress the idea of *contrast*.[5]

One of the most common figures and one of the easiest to use is *simile*. It is a direct attempt to relate two things of different classes by actually saying they are related. It is the portrait of a painter. In making the statement, words such as *like, as, similar to* and *resembling* are used as bridges. Thus, drawn from popular speech, we commonly hear: "good as gold," "sharp as a tack," and so forth. Similes are designed to clarify and enforce ideas though the effect is less than is provided for by metaphors.

---

[5]Note the unusual flavor added to a concept when one uses the linguistic device of the oxymoron to emphasize contrast: economic luxury, cold heat, planned casualness, frenzied relaxation, bright darkness, etc.

The *metaphor* expresses a strong and direct link between things of a different class. It does not create a bridge; instead, *it makes the two things as one,* thereby creating a stronger bond. It is the portrait of a mirror. Notice the difference between the following pairs: John swims like a fish versus John is a fish; The Lord is like my shepherd versus The Lord is my shepherd. Thus, the metaphor aids understanding and produces a style of brevity and freshness.

Other forceful figures include *understatement* and *parallelism.* The former, by opposing the popular tendency toward exaggeration, calls itself to the listener's attention forcefully. The latter, clarifies and strengthens by offering ideas in balanced form whether between sections of a talk, between sentences or within the same sentence. So, one feels the impact of "cry if you must, yell if you wish, protest if it pleases you."

As with all other aspects of good thought and language, the best figures spring naturally out of the subject, the time and place and are varied enough to prevent boredom, confusion or monotony.

SUMMARY

Good speakers strive to make their messages clear and orderly by carefully blending logical and psychological approaches. The style of the message, including proper and sensitive use of words, sentence arrangement and linguistic devices, does affect listeners.

PRACTICAL REMINDERS

Propositions

1. Clearly organized communication is more helpful in directing listeners toward acceptance of the speaker's message than that which is not.

2. The specific order of the ideas presented must vary with the listener, time, place and circumstance.

3. Generally speaking, it is best to place the weakest arguments in between stronger ones so the speaker begins and ends on strong points.

4. Enthymemes are more common to effective oral communication than syllogisms.

5. Messages which fill a clearly defined need in the speaker will be more readily accepted than those which do not.

6. Messages which include evidence for the general conclusions are more acceptable than those which do not.

7. Messages which demonstrate the support of authorities well-known and respected by the listeners will be more effective than those which do not.

8. Messages which have conclusions explicitly stated by the speaker are generally more effective than those which have not.

9. Messages which make frequent use of simple transitions (first, second, another important cause is, etc.) are more effective than those which do not.

10. Humor is most effective when it is drawn from the specific audience and occasion. "Set" stories and jokes are less effective, but may be improved by adaptation to the audience and occasion.

11. No effective speaker seeks to cultivate one style to suit all occasions.

12. Messages are strengthened by effective use of metaphor, understatement and parallelism.

Exercises

Theme

Directions: In each of the following examples, the subject as stated by the speaker confuses rather than clarifies the listener's initial understanding. Write your improved version in the space provided opposite each example.

1. Democracy is the best form of   1.
   government.

2. The American way of life is   2.
   ideal.

3. Brotherhood is the key to   3.
   social living.

Order

A. *Directions:* Refinement and precision of thought are best demonstrated by the nature and extent of the sequences, categories and other relationships provided by the speaker.

Arrange the following names into as many groups as you can logically support:

Sammy Davis, Jr., Dwight D. Eisenhower, John F. Kennedy,
Frank Sinatra, Joe E. Lewis, Albert Schweitzer,
William Howard Taft, Nat King Cole, John Barrymore,
Primo Carnera, Galileo Galilei, Jonas Salk,
John Unitas, Jim Thorpe.

B. *Directions:* From the following list, select those words which are generic and those which are specific. Develop a plan which demonstrates the relationship of the words in each section.

    1. addition, nevertheless, and, but, also,
       contrast, thus, furthermore, summary,
       in fine, hence, moreover, so, consequently
    2. creeping, theft, lying, riding, running, crime,
       sound, singing, robbery, motion, groaning

Development

Directions: Test these enthymemes by providing the *unstated* portion of the thought.

1. I will pass the exam today because I have my lucky pen with me.
2. The Protestant religion should be abandoned since doctrinal unity is not possible.
3. I am a veteran, why must I work?
4. That team will lose the game because it has thirteen members on the squad.

Words

A. *Directions:* Make a record of the denotation of each word listed below. Note particularly how the denotation prevents confusion with a similar word.

1. aggravate — irritate
2. preservation — conversation
3. pestilence — disease
4. funny — odd
5. invent — discover
6. journey — walk
7. infer — imply
8. test — examine

B. *Directions:* Place the stress mark (ˋ) in the appropriate place to distinguish between the following pairs.

1. instinct — instinct
2. conflict — conflict
3. converse — converse
4. compress — compress
5. essay — essay
6. refuse — refuse
7. record — record
8. permit — permit

Composition

A. *Directions:* Rewrite each of the following sentences to alleviate the ambiguity.

1. While asleep, the service station manager discovered the employee and fired him.
   (Who is asleep?)

2. Julius and Ida have been planning a trip to Italy for two years.
   (Long trip or bad planning?)

3. Heavy ladies' sweaters, $18.95.
   (None for slim ladies?)

4. Pat was elected Queen and escorted to the festival by granny.
   (Who elected her?)

5. The Boys' Club has a director, two gyms with libraries and restrooms.
   (Strange arrangements?)

B.   *Directions:* Complete the following similes so you construct a new and clear understanding. Avoid Cliches.

1. As nervous as _____
2. As quiet as _____
3. As cool as _____
4. As obnoxious as _____
5. As stupid as _____

6. As talkative as _____
7. As generous as _____
8. As faithful as _____
9. As foolish as _____
10. As good as _____

C.   *Directions:* Some of the following linguistic devices are useless because their various parts are inconsistent with each other and they serve to create a confused image. Identify the following poor examples and rewrite them in correct form.

1. He reported that the backbone of the cold wave was broken.
2. Each employee is an active member of the mosaic of our company.
3. Fred is an important arm in the administrative chain of this company.
4. Al's always stepping on the toes of the channels of authority.
5. He made as much impact as a dewdrop falling on a sponge.

6. The waves of indignation, stitched by the actions of a few, went like a shot through the audience.
7. He liked to work and taking in movies.
8. Ted not only found an employee but also a friend.
9. His pay as retail clerk is much higher than a truck driver.
10. Marie's eyes are dark like a cow.

Readings

Arnold, Carroll C., "Reader or Listener? Oral Composition," *Today's Speech,* February 1, 1965, pp. 5-7.

Ayer, Alfred Jules, *Language, Truth* and *Logic*, New York: Dover Publications, Inc., 1946.

Brennan, Lawrence, *Modern Communication Effectiveness*, Englewood Cliffs, N. J.: Prentice-Hall, Inc., 1963.

Chapter 5

SKILLS OF THE SPEAKER:
Situation Analysis

Among many educators and lay persons there is a belief that time, place and circumstance have slight effect on persuasion or learning. Others feel the only thing that matters in persuasion or learning is where and when it occurs. Both positions are seriously overstated, but are contained in the earlier statement of Principle A:[1] The dynamics of oral communication result from the psycho-physical aspects of the immediate environment.

From the general experience of living, most people realize that the psycho-physical environment does play a significant part in shaping such things as attitudes, attention and memory. It is easy enough to recall the feelings when, as an adult, one walked into a schoolroom, a church or a country club. The feelings are not similar. Some bring back certain attitudes and expectations not a part of other environments. There is an abundance of evidence to support the contention that *where* one confronts a persuasive venture is almost as important as on *what subject* and from *whom*. Obviously, in the very informal instances, a judgment is made quite rapidly without elaborate preparation and analysis. Nevertheless, even under these conditions the speaker must decide the appropriateness of the subject, the probable effect of the available time, the nature and extent of distracting factors and so forth. Note the unconscious choice which leads a communicator to allow more time for chats with friends than with strangers; allows more time for loved ones than friends. Are not people inclined to communicate more frequently and at greater length with those for whom they feel a sense of trust, respect and care than with those for whom they feel only mistrust and questionable respect? Does the time and place add or detract from the impact of a message containing news of a death? A wedding?

---

[1] See Chapter 2.

A birth? A termination of duties? A transfer? A failure? Very often, all too often, the speaker contradicts or compromises his communication by offering it in an atmosphere which carries an impression of carelessness, friction, insincerity and indifference, which the listener correctly reads as a true representaton of the speaker's feelings.

Depth, color and width are often added to a message as a result of where and when the speaker chooses to deliver it. Often these added dimensions are strong enough to change the original evaluation of the message while at other times they serve to add strength to the original choice. Think, for example, of the possible reactions to a message which the listener discovers has never been delivered before ("I love you"), or has been delivered regularly by the same person to many audiences ("You are the best class I have ever had"), or is always delivered at a certain time and place by different speakers (exhortations by commencement speakers). Is not the metamessage in each instance different? Do not some bits of information detract while some add to the message?

One of the more important of the physical factors which influences listener reaction is *time*. Quite apart from the element of time which considers the immediate psychological state of both speaker and listener from the most informal communication (a pleasant "hello" immediately upon rising in the morning as opposed to no comment at all) to the more formal classroom situations (conferences and seminars), the impact of time helps or hinders the success of the activity. Among adult professionals, for example, most successful conferences appear to be held in the autumn months while those in the spring and winter tend to be less successful. This does not mean, of course, that successful conferences cannot be organized for summer months; it does mean that summer imposes more obstacles to success than other seasons of the year and the successful communicator must do something to overcome them. Is not this the feeling regarding school sessions? While there are many successful summer schools, students seem to do better in the learning situations organized during the other months. The more informal communications do not appear to be as affected; although, there is some reason to believe that even these ought to be conducted with an eye toward the impact of shorter attention span, ease of distraction and the like.

In like manner, it has been found that Tuesday, Wednesday or Thursday are better days for the more formal, complex or important communications. So, too, with the various hours of the day. People tend to be more alert, interested and motivated during the early morning and afternoon hours. Speakers should base their choice of time more on concern for listener capacities than on personal convenience. The best time appears to be from nine to eleven-thirty in the morning and two to four-thirty in the afternoon. If evening sessions must be held, seven-thirty to nine-thirty proves most profitable. These times allow the listener greater freedom from such natural handicaps as fatigue, hunger and boredom. It seems most unwise for a distraught husband to attempt a successful communication with his wife between five and six-thirty, particularly if he wishes a decision on whether they should accept a transfer to another town. Tired as he is, he must recognize the barriers of fatigue (she, too, is probably feeling the adverse effects of being active for nine hours) and distraction (getting dinner, small children underfoot) which automatically work against his success. It would be far better to wait until dinner is over, the dishes are put away and the children are in bed. An executive who calls a meeting for four-thirty on Friday afternoon must do much more to neutralize natural barriers than one who consults with his people between two and four on Thursday. The teacher who chooses to hold his classes during the noon hour must exert more profound and constant judgments than one who selects an hour free from inherent competitions. And so it is with all instances of communication. If it is to be successful, a communion, no matter how fleeting or important, should be held during those moments which the speaker knows to be ideal.

Finally, the good speaker must consider the influence of time in terms of the length of his communication. Considering the speaker, listener, subject and circumstance, should the message be five minutes in length? Ten? Forty? Indefinite? At times the length of the communicative experience cannot be predetermined. One hardly knows beforehand how long it will take to persuade a friend to accompany him to a ball game. On the other hand, the teacher knows that a specific class session can be only fifty or thirty or forty-five minutes long and he endeavors to work successfully within these artificial controls. Generally speaking, both communicators exemplified above would do well to remember the greater number of barriers imposed by longer messages. Since most people have untrained memories, are easily distracted and cannot follow long chains of reasoning, the speaker would do well to shape shorter messages which are both direct and simple. Messages which run longer than thirty minutes require much care and refinement if they are to be as uniformly successful as their shorter counterparts.[2] Occasionally, some persons can run to seventy-five minutes without having the element of time act as a barrier to their success. But this can rarely be accomplished by inflexible or insensitive speakers who are

---

[2]Thomas R. Lewis and Ralph G. Nichols, *Speaking and Listening* (Dubuque, Iowa: Wm. C. Brown Company Publishers, 1965), p. 35.

completely oblivious to the force of time. It can be accomplished only by those individuals who note that personal privilege and worth are revealed by their use or misuse of time.

Besides the element of time, the oral communicator must concern himself with the advantages and disadvantages of the *location*. The wise speaker realizes that certain subjects can be discussed in an elevator while others can not; that certain topics "clash" with certain environments, others do not; that some subjects are definitely enlivened by certain environments. In making his judgments, the speaker must consider the general location (indoor, outdoor, home, office, school, church) as well as the specific location within those general areas. Is the front porch better suited for certain discussions than the living room of the home? Is the secretary's office more advantageous to some communicative endeavors than the private office of the employer? Is an outside room in a facory or hotel better suited for seminars than one located on an inner courtyard?

The speaker should also try to select an area suitable in *size* to his audience. Ideally, a location is "just large enough" to accommodate the needs of the activity. One does not choose to speak to a group of twenty-five persons in an auditorium which seats four hundred. Neither does he choose to teach thirty-five students in a room designed for fifteen. Less obviously, the efficient communicator also avoids engaging in communication (particularly on certain subjects) with one individual while twenty others are crowded around him.

Next, each communicator assumes responsibility for all *accessory* aspects of the location which may influence the outcome of his efforts. Such things as lighting, acoustics, heating, ventilation and storage requirements may hamper or destroy rewarding communication. Two of the greatest barriers to communication are bad lighting and inadequate ventilation. Many studies conducted for industry have demonstrated the enervating effect on the average individual of insufficient, badly directed or surplus lighting. It is less important to have intensity illumination than to have light evenly distributed throughout an area. Whenever possible, lighting should be natural rather than artificial. Indoor locations must be adequate, also, in terms of ventilation if the speaker is to be successful. Hot stuffy, smoke-filled rooms are not conducive to energetic speakers or responsive listeners. But, then, neither are locations which permit the auditors to be exposed to cold, drafts or alternating periods of discomfort.

Finally, the communicator must be cognizant of the various possibilities for *distractions*. Aside from the harmful effects of bad lighting and ventilation already mentioned and the easily imagined barriers imposed by poor acoustics, one must also know of the impediments created by ambient noise. Microphone feedback, whirring slide projectors, scraping chairs, and side conversations should be as great a concern as traffic noise, road repair machinery or cafeteria sounds. Furthermore, the good communicator strives to remove or minimize those distractions which arise from poorly displayed models, improper and irrelevant slides, charts, maps or uncovered windows opening onto a busy thoroughfare or a wonderful vista. These matters may seem trivial but because of them, listeners may be placed under great handicap.

Having exercised careful judgment in the matters of time, location and freedom from distraction, the efficient communicator turns his attention to the more specific arrangements for listening. Seating arrangements for the listeners should go beyond the basic consideration of number. They should include a scrutiny of the comfort level (too much is more a detriment than not enough), traffic flow, need for identification (special groups or individuals) and other detailed requirements. More important, however, planning in the more formal situations should concentrate upon optimum order. Ideally, the participants in a communicative situation should be seated reasonably close together. Obviously enough allowance must be made for work needs and matters of comfort, but arrangements ought to eliminate empty chairs or empty rows between participants. Except for group discussions, listeners numbering fewer than twenty should be seated in a semicircular, triangular or rectangular pattern. When there are more than twenty auditors, classroom or theatre style seems to offer fewer problems. The principal factor in the selection of seating arrangement (not predetermined by room size, special programs, etc.) is the opportunity for easy eye contact between listeners and speaker.

Speaking arrangements are another important facet of the oral communicator's total concern. The need for platforms or lecterns varies with the proficiency of the speaker, the nature of the audience and the formality of the situation. Generally, larger audiences demand the presence of platforms, lecterns and other such arrangements. If there is much use of graphic materials, slides and other visual aids, a slightly elevated speaking platform is in order. In addition, a small table adjacent to the speaker's stand provides the speaker with a convenient working area if one is necessary. It is the speaker, also, who must make the provisions for unusual audio-visual equipment, management and movement of props, distribution of handout materials and so forth. On the other hand, in less formal situations and with fewer auditors, the good communicator moves away from special equipment and endeavors to get closer to his listener. And elimination of such physical barriers tends to do just that.

SUMMARY

The oral communicator must give as much thought to maximizing or minimizing certain elements of the psycho-physical environment as he does to the various arguments within his message. If he is sensitive to this need, he will attend to the matters of time (month, day, hour as well as length and sequence of message), location (including such accessory considerations as lighting, ventilation and acoustics), distractions, listening and speaking arrangements. As Hollingsworth asserted long ago:

> ". . . the 'atmosphere' of the meeting place is an important factor, and . . . is due to the joint effectiveness of two influences. One is found in the immediate physical or mechanical features of the premises; the other is found in the faint revival of feelings of the sort which members of the audience have . . . experienced in meeting places of each particular kind."[3]

PRACTICAL REMINDERS

Propositions

1. People listen more discriminately during morning hours.
2. Talks are less effective if more than forty-five minutes long.
3. Poor lighting and ventilation distract more than ambient noise.
4. Audience seating should be controlled by the speaker.
5. Listener response is affected by the physical site.

Exercises

1. Construct a checksheet designed to improve situation analysis.
2. How should a talk be altered when a physical site requires a standing audience?
3. What does the speaker do when listeners begin to fall asleep?

Readings

Brown, W. and Wong, H., "Effects of Surroundings Upon Mental Work," *Journal of Comparative Psychology*, August, 1923, pp. 319-326.

---

[3]H. L. Hollingsworth, *The Psychology of the Audience* (New York: American Book Company, 1935), p. 171.

Fraisse, Paul, *The Psychology of Time*, New York: Harper & Row, Publishers, 1963.

Furbay, Albert L., "Influence of Scattered versus Compact Seating on Audience Response," *Speech Monographs*, June, 1965, pp. 144-148.

Perkins, H. V., "Climate Influences Group Learning," *Journal of Educational Research*, October, 1951, pp. 115-119.

Schultz, Duane P., "Time, Awareness, and Order of Presentation in Opinion Change," *Journal of Applied Psychology*, August, 1963, pp. 280-283.

Chapter 6

SKILLS OF THE SPEAKER:
Delivery

The speaker who has carefully conceived, organized and developed his message according to the needs of his listeners can still fail in his communication by ignoring the problems of delivering the message. To minimize the barriers imposed by poor delivery, the serious speaker studies relevant aspects of rehearsal and presentation.

REHEARSAL

To experience proficiency in any human process, the individual must rehearse regularly, purposefully, systematically and realistically. This is as true of the process of speaking effectively as it is of writing, finding a square root or driving a car. The various acts which comprise a process must be carefully practiced until they are committed to the realm of habit. Again it must be remembered that mere experience does not provide a guarantee of efficient learning. In oral communication, particularly, if experience were the only ingredient necessary to proficiency, all normal adults would be effective speakers since they have had years of experience. The thousands of people enrolled in speech courses do not suffer from want of experience; rather, they suffer from the lack of scheduled, purposeful and realistic experience. To become proficient as a communicator (in the more formal situations especially), the individual must allocate part of his total schedule to the matter of rehearsal.

For best results rehearsals should begin four or five days before the actual performance. Anything less would represent haste and result in inefficiency. These rehearsal periods can be used most effectively if the rehearsal procedures follow certain basic principles.

Principles of Rehearsal

In keeping with the admonitions of psychologists and educators,[1] the rehearsals recommended here reflect the characteristics of being *regular, purposeful, systematic* and *realistic.*[2]

Regular experience (or training) in the form of rehearsals is the basic requirement for the acquisition of new habits. As applied to habits of effective presentations, the individual must plan on a number of distinct rehearsal periods. He must understand that five practice sessions spaced over a period of five days is infinitely superior to five practice periods crammed into a two-hour period. Moreover, he must understand that equality of action is also required. In rehearsing a talk, the speaker must repeat the same procedures or activities although, of course, always striving to perform them in better fashion. This is also true of rehearsals that result in major content or procedural changes. By the time the speaker has arrived at the practice stage, major changes should be avoided. If absolutely necessary, such changes should be restricted to the first few practice sessions so that the sessions closest to the actual performance will closely approximate the real thing. The principles of regularity, then, must apply to time and method of rehearsal.

Purposeful rehearsals are those which are undertaken with conscious effort. This is to say that mere mechanical drill is seldom of value for anything other than the simplest of mechanical habits. Unless the speaker is deliberately aware and appreciative of the significant aspects of speaking, he will not improve because the habits will not become fixed. What has been called "conscious awareness" might well be referred to as the ability to *experience and simultaneously witness the act of experiencing.* Retention is increased whenever the individual is aware of his act of experiencing and does something toward insuring the repetition of only the perfect actions or associations.

Systematic rehearsals are those which, in addition to being regular, demonstrate progressive order. In other words, instead of being exactly the same as the preceding session, each rehearsal period ought to be more advanced. Toward this end, the speaker should arrange his practice periods so that the closer he gets to the actual day of performance, the more like the actual performance his rehearsal will be. While the first sessions may include use of outlines, the last sessions ought to completely duplicate the final presentation.

---

[1] See H. F. Spitzer, "Studies in Retention," *Journal of Educational Psychology* (1939), pp. 641-656.

[2] H. G. Rahskopf, *Basic Speech Improvement* (New York: Harper & Row, Publishers, 1965) pp. 30-32.

Realistic rehearsals are patterned as closely as possible after the actual performance. Again, it must be remembered the individual learns best only that which he actually rehearses. Should a speaker rehearse a formal presentation by muttering to himself while riding to work on the bus, he will learn only to become proficient in muttering on the bus. The speaker should avoid continual interruptions, diverse practice situations, incomplete rehearsals, imperfect aids and the like. He should strive to practice in a physical and psychological atmosphere close to that of the actual performance. If nothing more, this kind of realistic practice will furnish the poise that usually accompanies individuals operating in familiar surroundings. Moreover, the presentation is effective in proportion to the degree in which the practice periods duplicate the conditions of the actual performance.[3]

Types

Rehearsals, of course, may be of various kinds. In this section, the concern will be with the merits of *individual* and *group* practice sessions. The ideal program for rehearsals makes allowances for the utilization of both types, with the former acting as the prerequisite for the latter.

During individual rehearsals, after the material for the presentation has been selected, arranged and refined according to the demands produced by efficient audience and situation analysis, the speaker must strive to make the ideas more a part of him. In both individual and group practice sessions, this is accomplished by the regular, purposeful, systematic and realistic rehearsals mentioned earlier. Nevertheless, familiarity with the material comes best during individual practice sessions where the speaker, without the distracting element of a listener, may feel free enough to read from an outline. This procedure helps to fix the sequence of ideas in mind by eliminating any errors introduced because of poor memory. The presence of an audience during initial practice sessions is often translated into a tendency to emphasize delivery rather than content. In individual sessions, the speaker must try to establish a close familiarity with the material and until this is achieved drop all other considerations.

The practice sessions ought to adhere closely to the principles of rehearsal stated above, adding the consideration of *recitation, repetition* and *rhythm* to insure learning. In this regard, the speaker should deliver all versions of the talk aloud; to retain the good habits which can

---

[3]See H. Woodrow, "The Effect of Types of Training upon Transference," *Journal of Educational Psychology* 18 (1927), pp. 159-172.

be gotten from feedback, he should practice by using audible recitation. This is extremely important. In addition to the benefits of improved articulation, volume, pausing and phrasing, pitch variation and so forth, the speaker who practices aloud receives valuable aid in timing. Unless delivered in the vocal manner similar to that required by the actual performance, the speaker will not have a good idea of the time required to present the talk even though furnished with a well-planned outline.

Advantages also accompany the wide use of repetition. Rote learning is most helpful when one is seeking to fix mechanical and uncomplicated acts, but it is also of use in rehearsing oral presentations which are comprised of many dynamic and complex activities. The speaker who has rehearsed the main ideas of a presentation a minimum of five to seven times achieves a good degree of content familiarity. But it is essential that the speaker emphasize the ideas rather than the words during those practice sessions. With the exception of certain key phrases and sentences, care ought to be exercised to prohibit unnecessary word repetition between practice sessions. In this way, the speaker can learn to utter the same thought by using a variety of words and phrases. At the actual performance he will not be confronted by the inability to think of "the one word" which describes his thought; he can choose among three or four alternatives.

More ease in learning is added by rhythm. In the extreme example of the jingle or singing commercial, one sees something of this added ease in learning. In like manner, poetry which has marked rhyme and meter tends to be memorized more rapidly than material not having these qualities. In most oral discourse there is an inherent rhythm which can be accentuated during the process of learning to improve retention. With extra care, the practicing speaker can create a rhythm out of movement from *one idea to another, from main points to subsidiary points, from one mood to another, and from variations in vocal emphasis.* Characteristic phrasing and varied lengths of pausing also afford opportunities for effective rhythm. However it is accomplished, rhythm properly used will enable the speaker to learn his material with greater ease.

Finally, individual rehearsals might be made more profitable by the judicious use of a tape recorder. If utilized, the machine ought to be set up so it requires no act of maintenance during the time of the rehearsal. That is, the speaker should not have to interrupt his practice to reverse reels, rewind tape or replace the microphone. The recording can act as a monitor to faithfully report errors in content and delivery which tend to slip by the speaker who attempts to listen to himself. Any corrections ought to be noted on the outline and note cards for subsequent rehearsals.

Although practice before a group appears to approximate most closely the conditions of the actual performance, it can work against effective presentations. In the first place, practicing before a group can instill in the speaker certain habits or attitudes of unreality which might interfere with proper adjustment to the ultimate audience. It is possible for the speaker to become very good at *practicing* (rather than *giving*) talks before groups. In the second place, most group rehearsals or "dry runs" place an undue burden upon a practicing speaker. As they are often handled, these "group critiques" devolve into personal opinion forums with certain critics crystallizing all that is negative. Nevertheless, when properly administered, the group critique does offer the speaker the opportunity for a "shakedown" situation. The best views of many minds are unquestionably superior to one mind. And only in an audience situation can the speaker really test understanding. When properly administered, group critiques can and do offer much help to the conscientious speaker.

But rehearsals are only preparatory. The ultimate test is the talk itself, the actual communicative experience for which all previous preparation was made. Certain concerns which could not be sufficiently defined to be fully rehearsed become, in the final presentation, matters which must be understood and controlled. Among these are the use of *primary aids* (bodily action) and *supplementary aids* (audio-visual material).

PRESENTATION

Oral communication is an incomplete act without proper use of *bodily action*. Posture, gesture, movement and voice remain the universal signs of speaking activity. Without them, speech would not exist; with them, speech is inextricably bound to man's basic nature. From the earliest times, man recognized the strength of this bond and sought to use it as an aid to his own progress. The primitive tribes of Asia, Africa and Polynesia placed as much emphasis upon the "seen" communication as on the "heard." The Greek civilization before the advent of Christ taught its young that proper management of the body was a continuing and important part of their total development as citizens. During the Middle Ages and the Renaissance, special study was directed to bodily movements as they applied to communication. Giovanni Della Casa, important Renaissance literary figure who helped to establish the civilized behavior patterns of the Western world, offered the view that:

> Polite people ought therefore to be mindful of the need for restraint such as I have described in their manner of walking, standing, or sitting, and in all that they do, in their gestures and in their dress, when they speak and when they are silent . . .[4]

One scholar found, as far back as the seventeenth century, that he could get closer to an understanding of his fellows if he composed his face and body parts to suit the habitual pattern of the people with whom he associated. In this way, he pioneered the thought that by adjusting the body to suit certain universal postures associated with love, anger, pain and the like, these very feelings or emotions could be called forth.[5] The necessary corollary is that, in proportion as the body is prevented from assuming such universal postures or patterns, the feeling or emotion will not be felt.

In the twentieth century, while the thought expressed above may not have universal support, the oral communicator realizes that man is still influenced by the meaningful actions of the human body — whether his own or another's. It is this very realization which underlies the concept of *empathy*. As used by most modern scholars, empathy refers to the universal human tendency to become involved in the actions and thoughts of another. Crying as another crys, laughing as another laughs, feeling the tenseness we detect in another are all common manifestations of empathy at work. While this tendency is more prevalent among the younger members of society, it exists in all. And to the degree that it does exist in all social beings, the oral communicator has available to him another avenue through which he can effect a communion of ideas and feelings. In addition to the message delivered orally, the speaker has the opportunity to deliver it visually as well. Aware of the need to unite these audio-visual messages, the oral communicator works to improve his use of such primary aids as *posture*, *gesture* and *movement*.

Posture, as noted in Chapter 1, is among the significant nonverbal clues to inner tensions, feelings and attitudes. Postures can be "friendly," "combative," "indifferent," "confused," and even "exhalted." One who stands before another as though the weight of the world were on his shoulders will obviously issue forth a metamessage which differs sub-

---

[4]Giovanni Della Casa, *Galateo*, translated by R. S. Pine-Coffin (Baltimore, Md.: Penguin Books, Inc., (1958), pp. 94-95. Note also the advice in Thomas Elyot, *The Governor* (1531); John Bulwer, *Chirologia* and *Chironomia* (1644); Francis Bacon, *The Advancement of Learning*, IX, 2.

[5]Tommaso Campanella (1568-1639) was the obvious forerunner of the James-Lange theory of emotions.

stantially from one whose body is alert and responsive. While there is
no one correct posture for all activities and for all persons, there is an
optimum posture for each person in each activity. Thus, while a short,
muscular person may find it convenient and helpful to stand with his
weight distributed unevenly (more on one foot than on the other), a
taller person doing the same thing will appear ungainly and will draw
attention away from his oral message. To be efficient, posture must
contribute rather than detract from the communicator's message. Posture
which permits the speaker to be free for gesturing and movement without each time demanding dramatic adjustments is efficient.

Gesture, as with posture, is a basic part of the individual's personality since it is tied to early patterns of neuromuscular activity. The
feeling is that although gestures may mislead the listener, they do so
less often because they are more deeply associated with the real nature
of the individual. Just as penmanship tends to reveal hidden aspects of
personality, so gestures during the act of oral communication furnish
significant clues to one's inner traits. In any given situation, one person
may laugh, another may twitch and another may cough. Because of
Puritan etiquette and distorted emphasis on the use of gestures, most
Anglo-Saxons have been taught to suppress or diguise their gestures.
Such training has helped develop the "unconscious hypocrites" whose
words and actions do not coincide. It has helped, also, in the maintenance of a paradoxical attitude in most listeners who have been taught
that one can speak efficiently without gestures, but who continue to
feel uneasy when forced to participate in prolonged "blind" communication. When they are prohibited from viewing the speaker with the
necessary eye contact, the general reaction is to become less and less
interested in the message.

Efficient gestures are those which are (1) suitable to the communicator, (2) not distracting and (3) not sustained. Unfortunately,
there exists today many persons who feel that "training in gestures" is
the easiest and fastest way to improve as a communicator. Underlying
this belief is the idea that all persons should be trained to make the
same gestures in similar situations. If, as has already been discussed,
gestures are usually an inherent aspect of an individual's personality,
attempting to alter one's pattern of gestures may be an attempt to
alter one's personality. While this is, at times, advisable, it should not
become standard practice. The tall person is structurally suited to certain
types of gestures and unsuited to others. The person raised in an environment which stressed careful and sensitive body movements would
find it most unnatural and distressing to assume a pattern of flam-

boyant actions. As stated in Principle A,[6] effective speech is also selectively particular — this applies to gesture patterns of the speaker
as well as to special demands of the listener and occasion.

On the other hand, if one's normal pattern of gestures includes certain aspects which are distracting, then they should be minimized or
eliminated. Persons who have a habit of smiling indiscriminately, those
who automatically "stab" their points home and always in the same way
must work to eliminate or modify such gestures. It goes without saying
that certain gestures which are distasteful and obviously unpleasant
should be replaced as soon as possible. But simple things such as scratch-
ing one's head, ear or nose, putting one's hand in a pocket or wiping
perspiration from one's brow need not be avoided unless they become
habitual. A speaker who fights to suppress his tendency to do these
things as he feels the need will inevitably add to his feeling of tension
and thereby interfere with his own effectiveness.

But even these simple and normal gestures, if sustained, can become
distracting. A speaker who continually places and replaces his hands
in his pockets will decrease his effectiveness as will one who continually scratches his nose or loosens his tie. In short, gestures of consequence are those which are familiar, transient and spontaneous.

Equally important in the consideration of bodily gesture is the matter of eye contact. Long considered to be "the mirrors of the soul," the
eyes provide most observers with information relative to the speaker's
sincerity, good will and flexibility. Most listeners tend to eschew speakers
who refuse to look at them. The feeling is generated that the communicator is "not to be trusted" or that he does not really "care for
his immediate listeners." A simple experiment will serve to prove the
point. If, with the very next person encountered, one would carry on
a legitimate communication *while maintaining a fixed stare* at the listener's left shoulder, the nature of the interference mentioned would
be made clear. Discriminate eye contact sends forth a feeling of care
and concern for the immediate audience as opposed to a generalized
and abstract responsibility revealed in memorized manuscript or "canned" speeches which encourage fixed or "glassy" eye behavior.

From a concern with these more limited types of bodily action, the
wise oral communicator turns to a study of the role of movement in
speech. As with posture and gesture, there exists no single pattern of
movement applicable to all persons in all situations. Yet, many of the
financially successful charm schools and private institutes train their

---

[6]See Chapter 2.

students to adopt some such pattern. The alumni of such courses can be identified by their stereotyped activity ranging from three paces forward at the beginning of new points in their messages to one step sideward when presenting a new example. What both students and instructors fail to realize in such instances is that *patterns of any kind lose their effectiveness in proportion as they become standard or universal.* With movement, as with gesture, the conscientious communicator works to free himself of the belief that it is automatically to be avoided. He concentrates on recognizing his own patterns and moves to eliminate those which are distracting or sustaining. In the end, he recognizes that discriminate movement relaxes the listener and relieves the speaker of tensions generated by a static position.

To this point, the discussion has concentrated on the speaker's effective use of such primary aids as posture, gesture and movement. A word must now be said about the remaining aid contained within the speaker: *voice.*

If physical movement is inherently tied to one's real personality, then his voice must be even more so since it depends on such physical activity. The human voice, it will be realized, can hardly be produced by an inert, totally paralyzed person. As the individual removes himself further and further from the complete state of paralysis to the ideal state of alertness, his voice becomes a true "sign of life." Without any training in the matter, most individuals use voice as an index to another's personality, as has been mentioned in Chapter 1. If one encounters a comely female carefully groomed and tastefully dressed, his first impressions would probably be favorable. But if, upon speaking, she revealed a harsh and metallic voice studded with misarticulations and obsolete pronunciations those first impressions would tend to be replaced. Friendliness, aggressiveness and general emotional stability are revealed by the quality, pitch, volume and rate of one's voice. And, as with the more overt bodily action and as revealed by Principle C, modification of unpleasant or ineffective vocal qualities probably means a modification of the deeper personality factors underlying these qualities. But personality changes of this sort are not always necessary since indifference, fear or lack of training often accounts for distorted and ineffective vocal qualities. In most cases, it is enough to have a strong desire to understand what is involved and to improve.

Aside from cases in which definite pathology is involved, the most fundamental requirement the oral communicator must meet regarding voice is its responsiveness, audibility, intelligibility and pleasantness. It should be flexible and vital, easily heard and understood by the auditors and free from unpleasant elements. In other words, the speaker's *quality, pitch, volume* and *rate* must be coordinated in each act of oral communication if it is to be successful; to the degree that one or the other is warped, defective or inappropriate, good communication is impaired.

The unique quality of one's voice is shaped by the structure and use of certain parts of the body. The size, shape and lining of his resonating cavities and the nature of his bones and muscular system all help define the characteristic quality which in turn helps others identify him. If the resonating cavities are small and the bone structure is light, the quality (or tone, or timbre) will tend to be lighter and higher than if the opposite conditions prevail. Swollen lining (due to infections) and tense vocal muscles will produce more modifications. At the expense of oversimplification, it can be said that most problems of nasality, hoarseness, breathlessness or uncertain voices can be aided immensely (if not solved completely) by more purposeful and discriminating use of the cavities and muscles involved in voice production. As people get older, there is a tendency to restrict the jaw movements associated with effective use of the resonating cavities. Continued and purposeful practice, as mentioned in the earlier section of this chapter, in exaggerated jaw, throat and lip movements will help prevent the tendency from becoming a habit. Also, under certain psychological stresses, the human voice changes significantly. If this becomes habitual or even quite constant, the quality of the voice will become fixed as the muscles and organs find it increasingly easier to fall into these patterns of action. Hence, variety in mood and flexibility in use of vocal organs and muscles are the best insurance for a voice with a pleasant and effective quality.

Next to quality, the most recognized element of one's voice is pitch. Pitch involves the individual's ability (or lack of ability) to raise and lower his voice as compared with the established sounds of a musical scale. The good communicator evidences a range of at least one octave (eight notes) on the musical scale; the average communicator restricts his range to approximately four or five constant pitches and has a natural pitch located usually at one end or the other. Pitch changes are determined primarily by changes in the length and tension of the speaker's vocal folds and secondarily by the degree of tension throughout the rest of the muscular system. The most effective speakers are those who can control their vocal folds and reduce the amount of unnecessary tension throughout the rest of the body in order to utilize a great and continuous variety in pitch. It is through such variety, through the absence of a monotone, that the important inflections and modulations involved in clear meaning are produced. However, if such variety becomes constant, then the individual reveals a circumflex pattern of

inflection (often attributed to immigrant Scandinavians when first learning English phonetics). As with a monotone (or absence of variety),
the circumflex inflection (singsong) can be a deterrent to successful
communication since it calls attention to itself. Suffice to say at this
point that, excepting serious cases stemming from physiological causes,
pitch problems can be overcome by most individuals who communicate
with Principles A, B and C in mind.

Regardless of the idea or feeling, unless an auditor hears (or sees)
it, there can be little influence exerted by it. To most people, oral symbols are much more than sounds. They are, in fact, a kind of physical
contact. They can soothe, agitate, frighten. The whispering, harmonious
qualities of lullabies and the harsh, staccato, loud nature of most curse
words indicate this phenomenon. Loud words, acting as aural gestures
affect the adrenal glands, quicken the pulse, interrupt the breathing
pattern and so forth. For this reason, one's characteristic voice volume
should reflect the same viability as in pitch. The strength needed for
strong voices is dependent on proper control of the breath stream during
the exhalation phase of respiration. This control, in turn, is affected by
efficient use of the abdominal muscles, the diaphragm, the muscles of
the chest, back and throat. Increased tension in the abdominal muscles
coupled with a relaxation of the diaphragm and selected muscles of the
chest compress the lungs and force the breath stream against the vocal
folds with enough force to increase the volume. Unless the oral communicator varies the volume of his voice in response to his intended
meanings in a certain place, at a certain time and with certain listeners,
the full effect of his message could easily be compromised.

The speaker's rate of speech, the number of words he speaks per
minute, also carries an impact which may add or detract from the
success of the communicative experience. A rate which is above the
normal range of 150 to 185 words per minute will prove difficult to
attend and inefficient in terms of goals achieved (unless one's purpose
is to agitate, confuse and unnerve another). On the other hand, speech
which is below the normal rate can be equally irritating and confusing.
Thus, as with most other aspects of the entire speaking process, the
key ingredient in an efficient rate of speech is variety. At times, because
of the nature of the listener or the subject or the occasion, a slower rate
is better even than a normal one (when speaking over a public address
system in a very large auditorium). At other times, a faster rate achieves
the desired end sought by the speaker (when seeking to divert attention). Normally, the full range is used in rhythmical fashion.

Rhythm in good communication is probably the least appreciated aspect of persuasion. Yet it is so much a part of the naturalness of man

that its absence may easily result in the rejection of the speaker or his idea. While it may not be instinctive, the sense of rhythm lies deeply embedded in the human organism. Man is essentially a symmetrical animal, a bilateral structure with two brain hemispheres rhythmically controlling opposite sides of the body; a heart beating in rhythmical pattern (which when interrupted leaves the individual uncomfortable); a rhythm which accompanies ingestion and excretion, sexual functions, waking-sleeping patterns and many other phases of normal existence. Perhaps because of this internal rhythm, man expects rhythm in his external environment as well. He observes it in patterns of day and night, of seasons, of birth and death and even in his linguistic activity. Note that rhythm forms his incantations, prayers, blessings and lullabies and, in its absence (stuttering, spastic jerking, cacophony), he is disturbed. It is felt, heard and seen and because it is, it tends to be a requirement for successful oral communication.

Rhythm in speech reveals the true individuality of the speaker. How he moves from syllable to syllable (sensitively or indifferently), from word to word in casting his sentences, from thought to thought in forging his arguments and from mood to mood in giving special meaning to the whole, encourages or discourages listener participation.

Good speakers are also aware of the advantages and disadvantages of using *audio-visual material*. Aside from inadequate audience analysis, the most common error in more formal talks is the misuse of such material. The belief has grown that success is assured in proportion to the number of aids employed. The available evidence indicates that wise use of certain aids does help the speaker's cause. These aids, properly designed and used, clarify meaning and increase understanding.

When properly designed, audio-visual material is *drawn from the message*. Aids prepared and used by other speakers for other occasions are to be shunned. To be effective, aids must be patently related to the message and the audience. Further, they should be constructed after the talk has been organized and only for those sections needing more clarity and emphasis.

When properly designed, aids are *suited to the occasion*. Assuming that material is to modify listener behavior, it should be constructed so it falls within the range of listener experience. Furthermore, it must be familiar to the speaker and appropriate to the time and place of the communication. Cartoons for adult audiences and tape recordings of poor quality, for instance, can rarely be defended.

When properly designed, aids are *technically adequate*. To improve the communion between speaker and listener, the audio-visual material must be heard and seen by the communicants. Too often, aids are made by artists inexperienced in oral communication and used by speakers who, insensitively and carelessly, judge the adequacy of an aid by their own ability to see or hear it. Aids should be tested in the actual physical setting in which they will be employed, or one similar to it.

When properly used, aids reflect care and concern for the *needs of the listener, the occasion and the speaker.* This attitude is best demonstrated in the preparation and the presentation of the material. Regardless of form, the material should be brought into view only as it becomes a part of the immediate discussion. It must be covered or removed when not in use so distraction may be minimized. Also, all aids ought to be positioned beforehand to prevent needless waste of time during the presentation and to allow both speaker and listener to view them with minimal interruption of eye contact, unnatural changes in position or other adjustments which undermine effective communication. Finally, the aids must be timed properly so they do not occupy more than thirty per cent of the total time of the talk.

Despite popular opinion to the contrary, no one aid is perfect. Good speakers retain a flexible and critical attitude toward all such material and realize that efficiency varies with speaker, listener and occasion. Still, certain demonstrated advantages and disadvantages of the more popular forms ought to be known.

Among mechanical aids (those requiring mechanical equipment), movies have a high degree of popularity because they are easy to use, economical of time and unique in format. Films allow for observation of matters generally unavailable to the naked eye — growth phenomenon, complex coordinations of color, sound, action and so forth. Nevertheless, films can be disadvantageous when they dominate the communicative experience. For this reason, they must be carefully previewed so their relevance can be ascertained and highlighted. Unless the film is self-contained, the speaker should allow some time for discussion after its showing. Finally, the inflexible nature of time and content demand that the film be used as a unit or not at all.

Slides are not so inflexible. They are, moreover, easy to produce, use and adapt. They benefit the auditor by encouraging attention and increasing retention. They benefit the speaker by allowing him to use material (maps, graphs, tables) which may be too large or too small in its original form. Furthermore, slides help the speaker by allowing him to unify attention and direct it to areas he feels are important. But caution must be used to prevent poor quality (too much text or color, too elementary) and poor quantity (too much). An effective rule is one slide (if needed) for every five minutes of presentation, shown as needed rather than as part of a block before or after the talk.

Projections (opaque or transparent) are even more flexible. With these, the speaker is free to use a more spontaneous approach; maps, charts and pictures found in available texts can be used in their regular forms without the special expenditure of time, money or effort. Transparencies permit, in any sequence desired, the construction of charts and diagrams as the speaker progresses. Moreover, he can use projections without breaking eye contact with his audience if he is careful in selecting the number, frequency and kind to be used. In particular, he should avoid using typewritten transparencies since they are too light, too uniform and too familiar to impress most people.

Recordings have gained wide support within the last decade because more material is available and what is available is easily usable, and adaptable and is dramatic in effect. With careful use, the wise speaker can strengthen his effort by creating certain moods and by using the thoughts and voices of authorities respected and admired by the listeners. But as with other aids, recordings must be used in accordance with the general rules noted. They must also be previewed, introduced and concluded by the speaker and tested under the same amplification as required during the final talk. Finally, in the event of mechanical failure, the speaker should be prepared to use the contents in the form of quoted material.

Aside from the mechanical aids, certain display material should be considered in any discussion of audio-visual aids. Like mechanical aids, displays must be used wisely. The size, form, color, number and placement of labels, the progression of text and so forth must be carefully controlled by the speaker.

Maps, as a sample of this material, have as their chief function the graphic representation of distance, direction, location, size and the like. The use of maps as supplements to oral communication is strengthened with the use of overlays and three dimensional forms, but weakened by excessive size, color and detail.

Charts are used in order to highlight simple relations and total impressions and are proven most effective when they demonstrate simplicity and clarity. The "strip tease" chart by providing for an item by item revelation carries the greatest impact since it incorporates the unfolding feature mentioned in Chapter 1.

Graphs are best employed to represent statistical interpretations. Line graphs are best for indicating trends; bar graphs for quantitative relations; pie graphs for proportional relationships. In each instance, discreet cartoons and pictures can be used to highlight the relationships shown.

Writing boards, quite popular in industry and education, include such things as flannel and magnetic boards, flip charts and blackboards. Simplicity is the great strength and an indispensable requirement. These props also take advantage of the "unfolding" phenomenon since information can be revealed bit by bit as the speaker progresses. Important also is the flexibility which permits the visualization of concepts developed or developing in the immediate situation — if the speaker avoids crowding, poor handwriting, excessive speed, incomplete diagrams and so forth.

Models (including dioramas) permit the display of items and relationships which are too large, too small or too complex to be placed on one dimensional material such as slides and transparencies. Working models, of course, have the added advantage of movement but must be *used only as an aid* and not for *matters of interest*.

A complete understanding of audio-visual material used as aids in the communicative process can only be touched on in this book. It should be remembered though that the aids are only as good as the care and concern shown in their planning and use.

SUMMARY

While practice does not make perfect, a regular, purposeful, systematic and realistic rehearsal pattern will improve any person's ability as a speaker. One may practice by himself or in the presence of a carefully selected group. In either condition, one must apply recitation, repetition and rhythm.

Bodily actions can help or hinder his communicative endeavors. His posture, gesture and movement aid him and the listener when they are properly executed. In like manner, the efficient speaker may wisely use various supplementary aids in the audio-visual field. If these aids are directly related to the message, suited to the occasion, technically adequate and properly employed they can furnish significant assistance. Mechanical aids (movies, slides, projections, recordings) as well as display aids (maps, charts, diagrams, boards, models) have certain advantages and disadvantages which the speaker should know. The basic philosophy governing the use of audio-visual material is that if lost after they have been constructed, the speaker should be able to continue his talk without them.

PRACTICAL REMINDERS

Propositions

1. Only perfect practice makes perfect.
2. Group rehearsals are best after private ones.
3. Posture, gesture and movement must suit the speaker's personality, and subject and the occasion.
4. Eye contact is a help in communicating with strangers.
5. Good speakers manifest rhythm and variety in their voices.
6. Properly designed and used, audio-visual material provides the speaker's communicative efforts with strength, color and depth.

Exercises

1. Try to conduct daily activities without the spoken word. What areas offer the most difficulty? Which are least affected?
2. Go through the actions involved in shooting a pistol, a rifle, a bow and arrow and a slingshot. Practice for ease and clarity of action.
3. Without voice, describe a blood relationship (brother, sister), a need for a fifty dollar loan, a preference for hot dogs or eggs.
4. Repeat precisely and rapidly: Lester likes lemons lovelier while Peter prefers peppers peeled; tan cotton candy clean cold combs.

Readings

Davitz, J. R. (ed.), *The Communication of Emotional Meaning*, New York: McGraw-Hill Book Company, 1964.

Fromm, Eric, *The Forgotten Language*, New York: Henry Holt & Company, Inc., 1951.

Hall, E. T., *The Silent Language*, New York: Fawcett World Library: Crest, Gold Metal & Premier Books, 1959.

PART III

ORAL COMMUNICATION
Action and Reaction

We Listen Through a Screen
of Personal Experience.

"A Photographer Looks at Himself,"
Vytas Valaitas, Photographer

Photography Annual, 1960.
Used by permission.

Chapter 7

SKILLS OF THE LISTENER:
Preparation

UNDERSTANDING THE NATURE OF LISTENING

Effective listening is an activity which presupposes a precise degree of coordination in a sensory system which can receive aural symbols and an intellect which moves from symbol to message. Indeed, it is a manifestation of an even more profound co-ordination between two complex human beings — a purposeful, controlled and alternating silence. Silence usually acts as the leveling agent, the common denominator in a communicative situation and must be broken to establish individuality or true communion. In purposefully and systematically breaking silence, the communicants co-operate in creating social beings out of individual entities. In miraculous fashion, they each contribute toward directing the nature, scope and speed of "unfolding" their intimate selves, their interiorities. As Balzac observed in his youth, the listening experience creates an opportunity for a true communion.[1]

Listening is as important to the human personality as protein is to the human body. In the absence of this ability — as a result of either physical or psychological deficiencies — the human personality develops in a warped fashion. The inability to participate in the act of communication usually results in isolation, confusion, frustration and eventually madness. One can best see such responses in unfortunates who have been deafened by injury or disease, in the eyes of those who have been thrust into the middle of a conversation pursued in a foreign language, or in the activity of persons afflicted by the distorted and unintelligible sounds resulting from aphasia. Fortunately, advances in both research and training have brought the knowledge necessary to repair and develop the physical as well as the psychological aspects of

---

[1] Justin O'Brien, "Observer of the Human Comedy," *The Saturday Review* (July 9, 1966), p. 27.

listening. Man's current understanding of the process of listening goes far beyond the views published ten or fifteen years ago. Whereas he once was concerned exclusively with the physical aspect (hearing), he is now aware of the equally important psycho-linguistic phase; whereas once his focus was in assuring the clean and accurate perception of sound, his attention has progressed to the meaning drawn from that sound; whereas earlier concerns of education included training in the production and identification of the oral sounds of language, current views focus on increasing the nature and scope of experiences in order to increase understanding.

Most significant, however, new research in dissecting the listening experience has revealed it as a complex, complicated, mercurial but teachable adventure. Those who strive to improve their listening proficiencies now begin with the realization that the enduring and perennial problem is to keep various aspects of the experience separated (recording, interpreting, evaluating), to keep divisions of thought distinct and comprehensible while moving from one to another and to keep one's attention on main ideas instead of on the similar and related ideas which cluster about it and have no other effect than to weaken or confuse it. Sensitive listeners learn that the fluidity, flexibility and adaptability of oral communication serve to strengthen and weaken, help and hinder efficient listening.

Whatever their specialized emphasis, researchers and educators have been quite definite in underscoring the importance of effective listening in all phases of modern living. Most obviously, listening contributes to much, if not most, of our knowledge of our surroundings. Less obviously, listening offers a ready, universal and effective means of contributing to the social process of civilization. By enabling others to define their doubts, outline their confusions, register their protests, test their judgments and experiment with their dreams, the good listener furnishes the important catalytic force in the development of his fellows.

As with all phases of human activity, the trained individual is much more proficient than the untrained. Nuances are observed, precise coordination effected and general economy of effort revealed by the actions of the trained individual in everything from combat to communication, from letter writing to listening.

The trained listener is one who understands that effective listening in a communicative situation *is an active response to audio-visual phenomena which are employed in a dynamic environment for the purpose of modifying human behavior.* An analysis of the foregoing definition will reveal many of the subtleties which escape the untrained listener. Most persons who have learned their listening habits by osmosis assume that listening is a passive process, that listening can be improved by reading and that the listener is required only to be physically present, awake and reasonably attentive. In truth, effective listening demands an active auditor who is either taking notes, asking questions or contributing in some audio-visual way to the creative efforts of the speaker. It is in this way that the listener exercises his responsibility as a social organism by co-operating in the difficult task of maintaining a complex and dynamic relationship between subjective revelation and objective adjustment. With the co-operation of effective listeners, the speaker is able to measure his balance between the vertical axis (subjective concerns with self or between self and the Diety) and the horizontal axis (objective concerns with others) in his oral communication.

Effective listeners realize also that the process of oral communication is never restricted to forming, transmitting and receiving the oral symbols of language. They are aware of the less obvious but equally important super and sub structures which attend the more obvious symbols used in ordinary communicative situations; they are aware of the meta-messages discussed earlier. At times, for example, words actually are made to transcend themselves so they represent social gestures instead of personal conclusions. Such "extra structures" include the physical movements, or lack of movements, of the speaker (and to the sensitive speaker these same conditions in the listener), the time and place of the communication, the vocal reflections, the organization of the message and many more. Moreover, the well-trained listener is constantly aware of the dynamics of time, mood and various interactions of human personalities. He knows, as has been shown, that any communication delivered after lunch or late in the afternoon or just before dinner must be received with special care since his conditions of fatigue and distraction are greater at these times; that changing moods in the speaker must be reflected by greater flexibility in the listener. The obvious example of this kind of listening awareness is that shown by most good psychiatrists. But these same subtle appreciations are an important part of the listening habits of a good minister, doctor, teacher or friend.

Only the most naive individual would expect to exercise the same listening habits in both a formal lecture situation and an informal tête-a-tête with a girl friend. As pointed out previously, in each situation the overt purpose, the allotted time, the status factors (teacher-pupil vs. friend-friend) and the like all operate to demand various degrees and kinds of involvement. In some cases, his involvement is restricted to a silent re-creation of the images and feelings of the speaker; in some, he must urge or goad or evaluate by overt movements and audible questions; in others, he is directly and continuously involved by way of measured responses to the speaker's commands or requests. However, despite these variations, in each instance the dynamics of the communicative situation insure that *active involvement* will be the *sine qua non* of the effective listener (Principle B).

Finally, the best listeners realize that they represent the ultimate end for which each communication is designed. Good speakers keep this constantly in mind so necessary modifications can be made during the communicative act to insure the desired listener response. Good listeners, operating with this realization, exercise their responsibility for constant and continuing participation in creating, developing, modifying and evaluating the communication by establishing a purpose for every listening experience. To conserve energy and insure a successful experience, effective listeners begin their listening activities by deciding if the purpose of the experience is *entertainment, information* or *evaluation.* Few things are ever offered in communicative situations for no purpose at all. The purpose may be insignificant, hidden temporarily from both speaker and listener, simple or complex, but is inevitably present and serving as a directing force for both speaker and listener. Unless the auditor clearly defines his purpose and seeks to relate it to that of the speaker, he may gather confusion in the place of understanding. Many auditors have spent untold hours of time in abject disappointment and confusion only because they came prepared to be inspired while the speaker came prepared to furnish information. Professors, lecturers, doctors, lawyers, parents and friends have often been charged with negligence, incompetence and insincerity because the listeners expected one thing and were offered another.

One who determines that he enters into a specific communicative situation for the purpose of entertainment will not have to prepare in advance. When the pleasant passage of time is the only goal, the auditor involvement is variable in degree as well as continuity and he may laugh at a joke, talk to his neighbor in the middle of the next joke, daydream and so on. In a word, his responsibilities are more personal although his social obligations never disappear.

On the other hand, when the effective listener determines his goal to be that of gaining information (facts, opinions or interpretations), something more is required. Here, again, involvement is necessary to insure the success of the communicative experience but it is deeper and more extended than that required by the purpose discussed earlier. In addition to the adjustments which will be described shortly, the auditor who listens to gain information *must restrict his desire to evaluate the information in the process of gathering it.* The main objective is to record, not to criticize. What the speaker says is the most important phase of

the initial communicative encounter since the listener's reaction —
acceptance, rejection, interpretation, modification — is governed by it.
Consequently, accuracy in recording emerges as the desired goal of the
effective listener in an information-gathering situation.

Finally, one may listen for evaluation. Sometimes the situation is
such that the processes of gathering information and evaluation are
practically simultaneous. Time or circumstance do not permit the distinct separation of these activities and, more often than not, error and
misunderstanding result.[2] Unless they are separated, the average listener finds himself arguing with the first part of the speaker's statement
while the speaker is offering another part to modify the first. In this
way, arguments and decisions are based more on what the listener
imagined than on what was actually said.[3] Proper evaluation follows
information-gathering and does not begin until all the information is in
and understood. Thus, prior to a final evaluation, the effective listener
asks (1) What did the speaker say? (2) What did he mean? (3) What
is his degree of competence in the subject? (4) What is the nature and
degree of his prejudice toward the subject?

ADJUSTING TO THE DEMANDS OF LISTENING

Having decided upon his specific purpose, the listener must now
turn to the task of assuring maximum benefit from his listening experience by adjusting to the physical and psychological environments in
which his experience takes place.

While it is primarily the speaker's responsibility to select and maintain suitable physical surroundings for his communication, the listener
must share this responsibility by overcoming certain minor disadvantages. Among these is the matter of physical placement; that is,
the listener must choose a position (standing or sitting) which allows
him to see and hear the speaker with a minimum of strain. It is not
enough to assume that as long as one can hear the speaker he is suitably
placed in terms of his listening responsibilities. A moment's reflection
will call to mind the myriad instances where a speaker's mannerism defined the sub or super structure of his meaning and prevented a false
or misleading interpretation by the auditor. More than this, of course,
eye contact serves as an aid for the speaker. Unless the sensitive speaker
has the advantage of noting the facial expressions, bodily postures or
other physical activity engaged in by the active listener, he is unable
to monitor his ideas or the manner of their delivery.

---

[2]Rogers, *op. cit.*; pp. 14-15.
[3]*Ibid.*, p. 15.

Proper physical placement also includes a concern for adequate light, heat and ventilation. The stuffy, smoke-filled, dimly lighted room is not conducive to effective listening except possibly for the purpose of entertainment. Many studies by industrial organizations have demonstrated the unquestioned deleterious effect of insufficient, badly directed or — oddly enough — surplus lighting on the average person. In like manner, ambient noise drains attention and energy much more than commonly realized. It is more important to effective listening to have a constant, even distribution of noise and light than to have an irregular, inconsistent attempt to control either one. Erratic microphone amplification, outside traffic noise, kitchen noises and the like, if not taken care of by the speaker, must be adjusted to by the listener moving to a more advantageous position.

Another physical consideration, frequently overlooked, is the matter of time. Having a choice in the matter, the average listener ought to avoid important listening experiences which are presented during meal hours and in the late afternoon or evening. During these periods, the human body is besieged by internal stimuli which help to prevent or minimize listening effectiveness. Fatigue, unless dissipated by activity or replaced by nourishment, will interfere with sensation, perception and judgment. Most people, during such moments, tend to become irritable and easily distracted. This is also the case when auditors are required to attend presentations which are longer than forty-five or fifty minutes. If the speaker does not provide momentary diversion through controlled questioning, relevant humor or some other type of audience response, the individual auditor should provide for it himself. This can be done, most easily, by shifting bodily postures, increasing or decreasing note taking, asking a question of the speaker and so forth.

Finally, the careful auditor gives due consideration to his physical comfort as defined by his seating or standing arrangements. Obviously, too much discomfort will interfere with his concentration and, hence, ought to be avoided or reduced. On the other hand, believing that one ought to be as comfortable as possible is a serious mistake. Too much comfort discourages the motivation necessary for successful listening. In the vernacular it may be said that "if you ain't hurting, you ain't pushing." This applies to effective listening as it does to any other successful endeavor of life. Complacency has never been the hallmark of successful societies, institutions or individuals.

Aside from being adequately adjusted to the physical environment, it is necessary to emphasize adjustment to the psychological environment as well. Here, of course, the successful earwitness manifests continuing control of his emotional state. Personal problems are set aside (as much as possible) and full attention is directed toward what is being said. As mentioned earlier, the auditor should try to divorce *what* is being said from *who* is saying it until he has gathered *all of what is being said*. Often, all too often, misunderstandings are encouraged and maintained by the habit of half listening *or* nonlistening. Evaluations are made on the basis of the speaker rather than the idea, in terms of a party instead of a principle or in consideration of status instead of sense. While it is difficult to withhold such judgments, while it is more the rule than the exception to reject what the speaker is saying even before he has completed his thought, the successful listener does precisely this. And this he does because he is aware of the "unfolding" aspect of communication talked about earlier; he is conscious of the link by link development of ideas, desires and moods and, more often than not, of the listener's understanding of these phenomena; he is aware of his limitations which derive from his poor memory and his susceptibility for distracton.

SUMMARY

As it has been developed in this chapter, listening represents a human phenomenon which has physical and psychological aspects, individual and social consequences. It is an active response to audio-visual phenomena which are employed in a dynamic environment for the purpose of modifying human behavior. To engage in the activity with any measure of success, the sensitive listener strives to establish a purpose for each listening experience and then arranges his physical and psychological environments to contribute to a rewarding occasion.

PRACTICAL REMINDERS

Propositions

1. The responsibilities of speech are shared by the listener.
2. Most people are handicapped by poor listening habits.
3. Listeners react to speaker, message and occasion.
4. Active involvement is indispensable to successful listening.
5. Too much comfort hinders rather than helps the sincere listener.

Exercises

1. Arrange with some friends to have a speaker (a) deliver a short talk blindfolded or (b) speak to an audience facing away from him. Record the reactions which relate to the contents of this chapter.

2. During a class exercise (with the instructor's permission) respond to a classmate's talk by frowning, grimacing, shrugging, etc. When he is through, ask his reaction to this.

3. Arrange for someone to ring a bell (or give some other clear signal) five or six times during another's talk. At the signal, class members should record a "yes" or "no" to note whether they listened to the *idea being expressed at precisely that moment.* Total up the number of responses on either side to find out how attentive the class was.

Readings

Nichols, Ralph G. and Stevens, Leonard A., *Are You Listening?* New York: McGraw-Hill Book Company, 1957.

Rogers, Carl, "Communication: Its Blocking and Its Facilitation," *North-western University Information* 20:9-15, April 21, 1952.

Chapter 8

SKILLS OF THE LISTENER:
Participation

EFFECTING AN ACTIVE ROLE

At a time when man was developing his individual identity, when he was beginning to transport himself and his ideas with greater ease and frequency and when he turned his attention to founding universities, there arose a slogan: *Mors et vita in manibus lingua or* "Life and death rest in the hands of the tongue." The saying was, at once, descriptive and prescriptive; it told what society had observed to be a fact while at the same time it offered instruction to all sensitive and intelligent persons. It called attention to the fact that human speech may act as a sword, a shield or a lily. But more than this, while it urged for care in transforming experience into ideas and ideas into oral symbols because of their possible impact on another human being, *it presumed an auditor active enough to be affected.* To become misdirected, misshaped or otherwise harmed by the oral symbols directed at him by another human, the listener must perceive, translate and understand those symbols. What is not heard cannot be interpreted; what is not interpreted and applied can have only minimal impact upon the intelligent human being. At the base of every act of oral communication is the active listener (one-self or others) without whom the act of communication would be only a useless noise.

Listener activity may take many forms, but the most significant are those which involve recording and evaluation. As noted earlier, the natural tendency is to telescope these functions so they occur simultaneously. While this practice is the most common, it is far from the most efficient or the most rewarding. While this practice may be demanded, occasionally, by time, place, or circumstance, it should be avoided whenever possible. Each aspect of listening should be given distinct attention since it involves distinct and complicated demands from the listener.

Whether done mentally or in written form, the process of recording should be accompanied by definite and overt activity on the part of the listener. At the low end of the scale in regards to probable influence on listener learning are facial expressions, shoulder shrugs, smiles, laughs, nods, applause and the like. These indications of involvement are an aid to the speaker since they estimate his effectiveness. To the listener, such activities serve as reinforcements to interest as well as memory. It is as though he were "swept up in the general stream of movement, intellectually and physically. . . ."[1] To both, such active involvement furnishes a bridge, a bond, a link, a force whereby the socialization of individuals is carried forth.

The first requirement of recording what was said is the *structuralization* of the presentation. In most oral communication there tends to be more chaff than wheat, more support than thesis. The effective listener strives to grasp the central idea, leaving subordinate materials unattended except in instances where the main idea is not understood or is unacceptable. He does not become involved in details and is not distracted by examples, statistics, stories and the like. Moreover, he controls his tendency to embark upon tangential thoughts because he knows his task is to separate the main point from the mass of related though corollary ideas which can confuse and minimize. He reminds himself that, in proportion as the examples and illuminating details multiply, the initial thought grows fainter. He reminds himself, also, that he shares the human fault of poor and faulty observation.

Effective speakers consciously set the main ideas apart from their related thoughts by *pauses, increases* or *decreases in volume* or by *clear transitions*. Even poor speakers are inclined to pause slightly before and/or after stating what they believe to be their major points. On occasion, they might even combine that pause with a volume change to call the listener's attention to the idea. Both good and bad speakers make use of transitions — the linguistic signposts designed to inform the listener of turns, depressions, retreats and other variations in the stream of human reflection being presented by the speaker. The auditor who hears, "the most important thing to remember . . ." hurries to record it *whether he thinks it important or not*. After noting this (verbatim if possible), he allows himself a moment of relaxation when he hears such expressions as "for example," "for instance" or "such as."

Thus, properly executed, the listener's record of the speaker's presentation manifests itself in outline form with only as many details nec-

[1]Dominic A. LaRusso, "Visible Communication: Bodily Action," in H. G. Rahskopf (ed.), *Basic Speech Improvement* (New York: Harper & Row, Publishers, 1965), p. 219.

essary to provide him with an opportunity for reinterpretation or a final evaluation of questionable theses. No efficient listener (save the court reporters, stenographers and other specialists paid to do otherwise), attempts to secure a written or mental record of the entire talk. Not only is it impossible, it is completely ridiculous to assume that it is necessary to the success of the more common instances of oral communication. The most urgent consideration is a record of the major parts of what was said rather than what the listener thought was said, a record of the symbols shaped and presented by the speaker rather than those synonyms and substitute phrases provided by the listener.

If the sensitive auditor is moved to make a pertinent observation regarding corollary thoughts, contradictions, insincerities and the like, such short notations should be made in the margin of the notepad and put in parentheses or square brackets. Instantaneous impressions of the speaker's feelings, attitudes, pertinent items on his training and background which may be revealed during the presentation should all be recorded concisely and identified as observations by the use of brackets or some other similar device. In this way, what was said is kept separate from bits of information which may be used later in the process of evaluation.

Although related to the process of recording, the *art of questioning* is also a part of evaluation. However it is categorized, it is prominent enough to warrant a separate discussion. And any discussion of this basic aspect of man's intellectual pattern must include the obvious and traditional information regarding its use through the years.

Although indirectly a part of all traditions and a prominent part of the Biblical episodes, the art of questioning was given its greatest impetus by the antics of Socrates during the high point of Grecian civilization. In quest of his version of truth, Socrates felt the question to be more important than the answer since it served to define, direct and color the answer. He reasoned that asking such a simple question as, "Do you believe in God?" prescribed his companion's thought. Nothing could be said of sport, economy, politics or any other thing which the respondent preferred to think about at that moment. Further, Socrates thought it important to forge a process which minimized man's effort and maximized his reward by controlling his tendency to become involved in tangents. Accordingly, his practice focused upon shaping a specific question, gathering a response and from that response shaping a new question and, in turn, gathering a new response. His questions were always leading, based on concrete data, dependent on definitions and precise categories and, inevitably, moved from the known experiences of the respondent to the unknown. In this careful way, link by link, a literal chain of oral communication was formed.

Other great thinkers and teachers who followed Socrates, from Jesus to Mark Hopkins, placed a great deal of emphasis on properly-phrased, carefully-timed and sensitively-delivered questions. Any sensitive human and all successful listeners and speakers make the art of questioning a regular and continuing part of their communicative experiences. To do so, they operate with an understanding of the value, type and use of good queries.

As the name implies, the question starts both the speaker and the listener on a quest or a search for something which is not already a part of their immediate environment. This something could be a feeling, an attitude, an understanding or a bit of information which speaker and listener value enough to devote time and effort for its revelation. In itself, the question reveals an appreciation of another person — at least to the extent of realizing his presence. More than this, however, even the most trivial question reflects a degree of respect for another, a healthy lack of self-centeredness. Finally, the astute listener-speaker is cognizant of the indispensable role of the question in guiding thought, encouraging action and controlling the normal unfolding phenomenon of life.

But efficient use must also include an understanding of the various kinds of questions which may be fashioned. In the broader aspects, there are questions of fact, interpretation and value. Too often, the inept listener asks a question of fact, expects an interpretation in return and, when it is not received, becomes confused or incensed. More often, however, questions of value are asked under the guise of fact or interpretation thereby increasing the opportunities for misunderstanding. As with the need for separating recording from evaluation, the careful listener is aware of the need for divorcing questions of fact from those of interpretation and value. More important, still, the listener should not accept an interpretative answer for a question of fact or value. If one is offered, he should persist in gathering the answer he needs.

Within each of these broad areas — fact, interpretation, value — the listener must still choose among several forms of questions. He may, for example, ask open or closed questions. The former permits an extended answer as in the case where one is asked, "What is your opinion of Harry Truman?" The respondent is prevented, by the very nature of the question, from answering "Yes" or "No." On the other hand, the questioner may feel the necessity of asking a closed question such as, "Do you think Harry Truman was a good president?" While he may extend his answer, the implicit invitation is for a simple and direct response. In the course of a multisided communication involving several people, the listener may see the need for directing his question more carefully to a named individual. He may ask, "Dr. Miller, is it your thought that mercy killing is unethical?" In this instance, since the respondent was alerted first, he may be saved from possible confusion and embarrassment due to a momentary wandering of the mind. If the question was phrased, "Is it your thought that mercy killing is unethical, Dr. Miller?" the respondent may have to ask that the question be repeated. While other categories of questions may also be defined, the open, closed and name questions represent the most basic types and are sufficient for this discussion.

As with other things, a knowledge and appreciation of value and types are but the prelude to use. Proper use of questions is predicated upon four basic rules:

1. Make certain of the respondent's attention prior to delivering the question.
2. Keep the questions *short, clear, simple* and *definite.*
3. Be satisfied only with direct, relevant and complete answers (although you may deem it necessary to accept others).
4. Whenever time and circumstance permit, develop a progression of thought via a series of interrelated queries.

Fairly secure in the knowledge of what was said as a result of his active note taking and/or questioning, the concerned listener moves now to the process of evaluation.

When Professor Carl Rogers observed ". . . our research and experience to date would make it appear that breakdowns in communication, and the evaluative tendency which is the major barrier to communication, can be avoided," he was obviously underscoring the need for proper and timely evaluation.[2] Such an evaluation would begin with the message itself. It is at this point that the listener endeavors to go beyond what the speaker said by drawing upon his own training, experience and research to prove or disprove, to accept or reject. Having heard what the speaker said and having determined by reflection on the main points that he understands what he meant, the listener must next apply some of the simple tests of logic alluded to in Chapter 4.

Logic, as logic, is an intricate and involved discipline which involves much time and study. As a basis for successful evaluation of various oral communications, it can be greatly simplified without impairing its

[2] Rogers, *op. cit.,* p. 9.

value. In the first instance, since logic always involves a leap from one idea to another, the acceptability of the main point must be established; one must examine the idea from which the leap is made. This can be done, in simplest fashion, by trying to discover valid exceptions to that proposition. To the thought that "elementary level teachers are underpaid," the average listener can attach innumerable instances of incompetent teachers he has known who have drawn too much from public funds. By the same token, he can probably cite three or four teachers who make as much as professionals in other areas but work on a contract totaling 185 days. These exceptions serve not so much to argue for the rejection of the proposition as to call for caution in concluding that "we need federal aid to education." Perhaps federal aid is needed, but it should be based upon something more than the broad and questionable statement that "elementary level teachers are underpaid." On the other hand, the statement "we had a Puerto Rican gardener once so I don't think we should vote for the Puerto Rican candidate for Senator," is best tested (again by collecting exceptions) by demanding a broader base for the conclusion. The old adage that "one raindrop does not constitute a storm" should be applied to any attempt to make a category or class or general statement from one example. The second step should be to examine the idea to which the leap is made and in the same manner described above.

In addition to testing the idea *from* and *to* which the logical leap is attempted, the listener must probe the relationship between them to determine if it is what the speaker describes it to be. He must ask, for example, if the connection between the two main ideas is clear, direct and necessary. Can the transitional bridge between the major points be altered with as little or as much rationale as is used to maintain it? Can one change the statement "handicapped persons succeed *in spite* of their handicaps" with as much or as little substantiation as offered in presenting the first version? If so, then another reason for delaying the acceptance or rejection of the major propositions comes to the surface. By attending to the *function of the transition* used to connect the main points, the astute listener can also evaluate the acceptability of the speaker's logic. The speaker may feel that "John Smith is a poor teacher because he is from the East," but the efficient listener will make this as a conclusion which demands explanation. While each of the major ideas ("John is a poor teacher and he is from the East") may be true, one can hardly be connected with the other in a cause and effect relationship without explanation.

Quite obviously, the analysis of the oral message for logical soundness can be much more involved and protracted than the brief pattern discussed here. Specific and detailed questions are available which can be applied to syllogisms, statistics, analogies and the like in the endeavor to evaluate arguments. However, in the heat, fluidity and immediacy of most instances of oral communication, the average listener finds neither the memory nor the time nor the inclination to apply such extended tests to messages presented for his benefit. Nevertheless, in order to protect himself and exercise his responsibility to society, he should strive to apply some sort of analytic pattern to whatever he hears whenever he hears it.

Still, this is not enough. In the previous chapter, attention was called to a fact recognized by all successful auditors: In addition to the message itself, meaning is derived from certain nonmessage factors. These nonmessage factors have been spoken of before as constituting sub or super structures which accompany the oral symbols used. They include physical movements of the speaker, tone of voice, selection of time and place for the communication and the like. These sub or super structures, in effect, produce a metamessage; these added ingredients very often combine to produce another message — one which may be similar to or different from the more obvious message being delivered by the speaker. To evaluate the entire communicative effort, the careful listener must consider certain aspects of the metamessage.

Combined with the aspects of nonverbal communication discussed in Chapter 1, the listener should compare relevant aspects of the formal message *with* what he knows of the *speaker* and of the *time, place and circumstance* of *delivery.* If the speaker is personally recognized by the listener as a man of integrity, competence and good will it should be recognized that the message will probably "come over" encased in a predetermined atmosphere of acceptance. Right or wrong, most persons are influenced by the very nature of the people with whom they deal. In any walk of life, people are inclined to believe certain persons and to distrust others. From some, individuals are inclined to accept the biggest falsehood; from others, they are inclined to reject the most obvious truth.[3] Being aware of this tendency, in himself as well as in others, the responsible listener will try to identify the extent to which it has affected his evaluation of the message. He reminds himself repeatedly that no one is capable of creating masterpieces every time he works, regardless of his past reputation. Conversely, on occasion even the most ignorant person is capable of an irrefutable truth. The competent auditor tries to identify and separate *what* was said from *who* was saying it *at least until an evaluation on the basis of the relevance*

---

[3] S. C. Menefee, "The Effect of Stereotyped Words on Political Judgments," *American Sociological Review* 1 (1936), pp. 614-626.

and validity of the ideas is completed. This does not mean that it is always wrong to reject a message precisely because a particular speaker was presenting it. It does mean that each rejection for such a reason ought to be clearly identified so as to prevent the listener from believing his choice is based on more logical reasons. In sum, *the good listener forces himself to evaluate each message from each speaker on the basis of its merits.*

In addition, however, the sophisticated listener is responsible for noting the nature of the various metamessages sent out by the time, place, purpose and mode of communication. He makes himself aware of the message revealed by the speaker's choice of *when* to communicate, to *whom* and for *how long.*

The latest information drawn from the areas of psychology and psychiatry reminds us that very often, the vocal and bodily actions we employ or avoid employing reveal more about how we feel and what we think than the words we use. An alert earwitness recalls:

> . . . the obvious connections between bodily actions and illness, e.g., distorted facial expressions, involuntary movements (tics, blinking, twitches), uncoordinated movements of gait which accompany some states of health, abortive movements of stuttering. In less obvious instances, the habitual patterns of action employed by the 'normal' individual also reveal his state of mind. Random tapping, unrelated smiles, averted eye contact, constant shifting of weight, while they fall within the normal range of action, nevertheless convey meanings concerning basic personal adjustments to the world. In addition of course, such mobility, or non-mobility, connotes one's adjustment to the immediate situation.[4]

From all these things, the listener constructs the metamessage and compares it with the message itself to make his final judgment.

SUMMARY

To insure the success of his listening adventure, the auditor must become actively involved in the act of oral communication. He must focus his efforts on recording the speaker's message (and his metamessage) before he seeks to evaluate it. This recording is done best in writing but, regardless of how, it is most efficient and accurate when in outline form with special emphasis on the basic ideas. The recording as well as the evaluating process is helped by a discreet use of the art of questioning. The final process of evaluation includes a concern for the acceptability of the major ideas, the logical patterns employed to

---

[4]LaRusso, *op. cit.*, p. 223.

relate these ideas and the comparison of the message formed by these ideas with the metamessage given by the speaker as well as the time, place and circumstances of delivery.

The careful listener crystallizes his participation by seeking answers to (1) What did he say? (2) What does he mean? (3) What is his degree of competence? (4) What is the nature and degree of his prejudice toward the subject?

PRACTICAL REMINDERS

Propositions

1. Effective listening includes distinct processes of recording and evaluating.
2. Recording is best done in written, outline form and, whenever possible, makes use of the art of questioning:
   a. What did he say?
      1. Main ideas with relevant detail?
      2. Verbatim symbols not paraphrases?
      3. Listener's observations clearly marked?
   b. What did he mean?
      1. Did he speak irony, sarcasm, humor?
      2. Did he speak literally?
      3. Is there a metamessage?
3. Evaluating includes finding out:
   a. What is his degree of competence in the subject?
      1. Personal experience (training, education, work)?
      2. Nature and use of secondary sources (are they from competent experts, are they traditional, or are they common knowledge)?
   b. What is the nature and extent of his prejudice in this area?
      1. Is he a reluctant witness?
      2. Does he alter his known views for this occasion?

Exercises

1. How may the following questions be answered?
   a. Do you want to go? b. Pardon me, please? c. Would you mind passing the salt? d. Don't you believe that _____?
2. What does the speaker mean by
   a. prewar b. preschool c. preshrunk d. preheated
3. Have a friend observe your listening habits on several occasions of his own choosing when you are unaware of his observations.

Compare your reaction to each speaking situation with his record of your activity. Does any pattern emerge?

Readings

Broadbent, Donald E., "Failures of Attention in Selective Listening," *Journal of Experimental Psychology* 44: 428-433, 1952.

Jastrow, Joseph, (ed.), *The Story of Human Error*, New York: D. Appleton-Century Co., 1936.

Johnson, Wendell, *People in Quandaries*, New York: Harper and Brothers, 1946.

Mason, Harry, "Personal Values as Factors in Listening Ability," *American Psychologist* 4: 395ff., 1949.

Reik, T., *Listening With the Third Ear*, New York: Farrar, Strauss & Company, 1948.

Weaver, Carl H., "Don't Look It Up — Listen!" *Speech Teacher* 6: 240-246, 1957.

INDEX